5-MINUTE
RETREATS

for
*M*OMS

SUE AUGUSTINE

HARVEST HOUSE™ PUBLISHERS

EUGENE, OREGON

Cover by Left Coast Design, Portland, Oregon

Cover photo by Phil Hunt, Getty Images

5-MINUTE RETREATS FOR MOMS
Copyright © 2003 by Sue Augustine
Published by Harvest House Publishers
Eugene, Oregon 97402
www.harvesthousepublishers.com

Library of Congress Cataloging-in-Publication Data
    Augustine, Sue
        5-minute retreats for moms / Sue Augustine.
            p. cm.
        ISBN 0-7369-1236-3 (pbk.)
        1. Mothers—Psychology—Miscellanea. 2. Mothers—Conduct of life—Miscellanea. 3.
    Self-help techniques. 4. Relaxation. 5. Pleasure. I. Title: Five minute retreats for moms.
    II. Title. HQ759.A884 2003
        646.7'00852—dc21   2003002444

Dedicated to all the moms I know who have ever been found riding an antique merry-go-round, building sandcastles, jumping in autumn leaves, making snow angels, splashing in rain puddles, licking Popsicles, and watching fireflies twinkle in the night—with or without the kids!

CONTENTS

AH, THE GIFT OF MOTHERHOOD

*B*eing a mom can be the hardest, wildest, wackiest, most exhilarating, and fulfilling job you've ever had in your lifetime. But the one thing more moms wrestle with than anything else, is the feeling that taking care of their personal well-being comes somewhere down the list after fulfilling their other roles as wives and mothers.

Let's face it—once you have children, they're always around. They follow you into the bathroom, insist on coming with you to get the mail, and always have to tell you something *really, really* important when you're on the phone. You never get a break. It seems there is never enough time to get refueled and recharged. Establishing some mommy space and time away from your children plays a tremendous role in the way you interact with them. Longing to find some "me time" does not make you a horrible mother! It is not only a good idea to take time for self-nurturing, it is essential for staying true to yourself and carrying on with your family commitments and involvement.

In our culture, moms are often given the impression that in order to have an effective, enjoyable, and productive life, they must do it all—climb the corporate ladder during the week; work out at the gym every morning; go for a walk during lunch; do science-fair projects with the kids after school; cook healthy, balanced meals every night; be a wonderful hostess and entertain guests in the evenings; spend weekends making kettles of vegetarian soup and baking multigrain muffins; look great all the time; and if that isn't enough—turn into a sex goddess after dark!

While you do have a reputation for being able to do it all—juggling work and family while bringing home the bacon and frying it up in a pan—you also need a little time to yourself. A burnt out mom is simply not the best mom she can be. The truth is it's not only a good idea, but it is absolutely critical for you to carve out time to relax and recharge.

But how do you find that elusive "me time" so it can be reflected in the time you do spend with your family? It's not as impossible as it seems. By practicing *healthy selfishness*—keeping a balance between putting your family first and finding time to have your own needs met—it's possible to truly enjoy being a mom without sacrificing your own health, well-being, and peace of mind. After all, the whole family is happier if you are happy. When one little boy made the statement, "If mamma ain't happy, ain't nobody happy," he wasn't kidding!

This book is my invitation to you to make 5-minute retreats your lifestyle. Its pages are brimming with simple ways to make time for yourself to get the most from life. Now I know that some of these retreats don't fit the 5-minute time frame, but if you've picked this book up and are reading a suggestion daily, allowing your weary mind to take a mental break, there's hope for you yet! Simply thinking about some of these activities can be your retreat. You'll be amazed at how taking time for yourself is going to change your life. I pray these mini escapes will heal your harried heart and calm your frazzled mind so you can let go of stress, relax, and enjoy being a mom more than ever before!

PART 1

TIME OUT FOR MOM

YOU DESERVE
A BREAK

Who are these kids, and why are
they calling me mom?

nwind and take a well-deserved break!" There is always someone urging you to take some child-free time just for you. Maybe it's an article in a current magazine, your mother, a caring (probably single) friend, or the book you are reading at this moment. Even your husband is asking you to let everything go, turn off your mind, and relax (which would be wonderful if you thought he meant he'd take over while you do!). So how do you manage to a take a breather when you're already behind schedule, you can't find your keys for the umpteenth time, and to top it all off, you've got the worse case of the monthly, hormonal screaming meemies you can ever remember?

When adrenaline has become your main source of fuel, your hormones are out of balance, and you're literally running from one item on your to-do list to the next, peace of mind seems like an impossible goal. You'd like to relax, but you can't seem to slow down. Somehow life keeps getting in the way.

All moms have moments—or even whole days—when they feel they cannot wipe one more runny nose, trip over one more pile of building blocks, mop up one more sticky mess, or summon up the energy for one more rendition of "This Little Light of Mine." At these times, you may be thinking that the only answer is a one-way ticket to anywhere (no forwarding address) or a sports car that seats one and comes with a full tank of gas.

A more realistic approach *would* be to acknowledge that you are suffering from exhaustion and you'll probably collapse if you don't take a real break to do something just for yourself. Plan ahead and have some 5-minute retreat ideas on hand that you know will help you stay sane and revive your energy. For someone without children, these innocent escapes may seem trivial or insignificant, but for you as a mom, time is at a premium and even the most modest leisure activity can go a long way toward helping you through the turmoil.

You do deserve a break today. Tell your inner critic to *shush*, and remind yourself that you and your family will be better for it.

GO TO YOUR ROOM!

*When we do something for ourselves alone, we
send a signal to our soul that our
life has value.*

ALEXANDRA STODDARD

ost kids these days wouldn't object a whole lot to being sent to their room. After all, it's a place full of their special "stuff," with surroundings that are cozy and familiar. They have their favorite music and reading material, cuddly stuffed animals, fluffy pillows and cozy comforters, fun toys, craft kits, and art supplies they can use to keep themselves occupied, and also the space to simply relax and do nothing but think their own thoughts if that's what they choose to do. As a young mom, I remember thinking what a special treat it would be to be given a "time out" and to be sent to *my* room.

Moms do need a spot of their own—a special place to retreat to that is off limits to others. Children have their playrooms. Fathers have their workshops, garages, or basements. When moms do have a place, it's usually a craft or sewing room, or a home office; however, these are often public domain. A spot of your own should provide the privacy you need to catch your breath.

Most dads are good at this. They have their favorite chair and no one would dare sit in it! That's how it was growing up in my house. That is, until my two younger sisters came along who hadn't figured this out. They were much more rambunctious than their older siblings and while jumping wildly in Dad's chair one afternoon, they knocked his special reading lamp onto the floor. When the porcelain base broke into large chunks, they knew they were in big trouble. As fast as they could, they reassembled the whole thing by stacking the pieces together (without glue), and finished off the project by perching the lampshade back on top. It may have appeared to be in one piece, but later that evening Dad sat down with his newspaper, and as he pulled the chain to turn on the light, he watched in astonishment as the whole thing went crumbling to the floor! Needless to say, the girls learned to have a new respect for Dad's territory after that.

Just as fathers have their special chair, you deserve a small haven of your own. You might choose a spare room, a sitting room, or even a corner of the bedroom where you'll be undisturbed. It could simply be a much-loved chair or a window seat, but wherever it is, let others know it's off limits. Make your little spot a sacred place where you can go to spend time alone with God, read, ponder, and renew your spirit. Make it snug, cozy, and inviting. Decorate it with accessories you find relaxing and restful. Now it's up to you to go to your "space" and practice healthy selfishness—if only for 5 minutes.

TAKE A HIKE!

There is pleasure in the pathless woods.

ven with small children, it is possible to break away from everyone to get outdoors for a short hike. Without leaving home, you can meander up the driveway, down a garden path, or around the exterior of your house. If only for 5 minutes, stop what you are doing and get out by yourself. Depending on the ages of your children, do this while the kids are napping, working on a craft project, or watching a favorite video. If your children are at school and you happen to be alone during the day, take a coffee break or a few minutes at lunchtime to stroll down the street and back again. Practice shutting the world out, and get in the habit of praying while you meander. This is not about getting physically fit, but spiritually in shape. If your little ones cannot be left alone, walk together and turn your hike into a treasure hunt or discovery adventure. Sometimes stepping outdoors for a moment for some fresh air, whether alone or with others, is all it takes to restore a sense of serenity.

With my office at home, I had developed the habit of strolling to the end of my country driveway to the mailbox everyday at noon. When my grown daughter started coming to assist me with office work, she arrived just after the mail had been delivered and thought she would do me a favor by picking it up and placing it on my desk.

At first, I was grateful she was saving me the trip, and I thought it was a good idea…until I noticed I was starting to feel sluggish and out of sorts during each afternoon. I couldn't put my finger on the reason until it dawned on me that those mini-strolls had been giving me the break I needed to be a more creative problem solver. It also boosted my energy for the rest of the day.

When you do get out to saunter for a bit, you may find yourself doing some creative meal planning or perhaps you'll be able to rehearse ways to tactfully respond to an overbearing family member. You might find yourself deciding how you'll complete a discussion that was left hanging or maybe using the time to pray for guidance, for inner peace, for your family, for other moms. Ask for answers and then listen for the voice of God giving you direction and guidance. Outside, wake up to the world all around you and become aware of your surroundings—the scents, sounds, and textures. Notice the harmony of nature. Count your blessings and give thanks. We invest so much time, thought, and effort into being physically, mentally, and emotionally fit, but often leave our spirit out of the equation. Taking a walk, stroll, or mini-hike helps you get your spirit fit.

HEAD FOR
THE HILLS

*It's all right to take life seriously, as long
as you don't take yourself the same way.*

t a beautiful evening garden party I attended, guests
were seated in a circle on the lawn. I arrived late,
located the only remaining open spot in the circle, and
positioned my lawn chair very carefully because I noticed there was
a slight incline (clearing up any question as to why no one was sitting there!). Obviously I was not careful enough, because in just a
few moments, I could feel my chair sliding ever so slowly down the
hill. The more I tried to get my balance and stand up, the more I
kept slipping along with the chair. Eventually, I fell right out of the
chair and kept rolling until I got to the bottom of the hill. Of course,
every eye was on the rolling woman, and mouths were hanging wide
open in complete astonishment. They couldn't believe what they had
just witnessed! I knew I'd have to think fast because they'd all be
waiting for some sort of comment. I stood up, brushed off my skirt,
composed myself, and announced very seriously to my audience,
"For the benefit of any of you who may have missed tonight's performance, I will be glad to do an encore." Everyone applauded and I
had a good laugh, too. As Ethel Barrymore said, "You grow up the
day you have the first real laugh—at yourself."

Now, I'm sure I would have had a lot more fun had I not been
wearing a skirt, for one thing, and also if I'd been alone. I think I

would have just let loose and entered into the experience with total abandon, rolling to my heart's content. Do you remember doing that as a child? What I'm wondering is, have you done it lately? My guess is that you have not. Why not round up your children, or a friend in need of some spontaneous fun, and find the biggest, grassiest hill around? Then, stretch out at the top and let yourselves go.

When our first grandson, Kurtis, was a toddler, he and I would roll down the hill in our backyard. Kurtis wasn't really all that fond of my new pastime, but I'm the grandma, and I said let's do it. Later on, to be fair, I would take him indoors and we would work together on his favorite pastime—assembling puzzles. Having a child with me was a wonderful excuse to head for the hills. It's too bad we think we can't do those things on our own. So head for the hills and have some fun rolling to the bottom. As Margaret Deland encouraged, "As soon as you feel too old to do a thing, do it."

GO FLY A KITE

The heavens declare the glory of God.

PSALM 19:1

hen my husband, Cliff, and I were in Hawaii, an international kite-flying competition was taking place at a park within walking distance of our hotel. We decided it would make a nice outing on a Sunday afternoon after church, so we took a walk to the park. As we got closer, we could see the magnificent display of kites in the sky. We'd never seen anything quite so impressive. There were kites of every shape and size imaginable. Most of them were enormous and their radiant colors glistened in the island sunlight. Then, we gasped as we caught sight of the most amazing spectacle—a small boy wearing a baseball cap, laying on top of his kite and soaring high in the sky. Of course, I felt silly when I eventually realized it was a kite made to look like a life-size little boy. But for those few minutes, it had me imagining what it must be like to experience the freedom of flying through the sky like a bird. It reminded me of a verse written by the psalmist, "Oh that I had wings like a dove. I would fly away and be at rest."

There is something liberating about the thought of soaring through the sky. The mere experience of flying a kite has a way of setting the soul free as though you were being carried toward the blue sky. As you run across an open field, or stand high on a hill with the wind blowing through your hair and your kite is resting on the underlying currents of air, rising effortlessly heavenward, it's easy to close your eyes and imagine you will be lifted up from the earth at any moment.

Think of how enjoying the wind can be a retreat for you. I own a convertible and the best part for me is feeling the wind blow wildly through my hair. At one time, I would have hunkered down and bundled up if someone were to open the car windows, especially if my hair had just been styled and sprayed. Now, having my hair mussed is the furthest thing from my mind.

When was the last time you felt the wind in your hair? Was it during a ride on the roller coaster at an amusement park or the time the car windows were stuck and wouldn't go all the way up? Maybe it was while you were riding a bicycle or perhaps on vacation at the beach. Maybe it's been far too long since you've experienced that kind of total windblown abandonment.

Think of places you could go to enjoy the wind—standing on a bridge, at the top of a hill, on the balcony of a tall building. Seek out opportunities to feel the wind on your skin and blowing through your hair. On the next windy day, go outside and enjoy the sheer sense of liberation that the wind brings. Hang a windsock or flag outside your door. Buy a child's windmill on a stick. Purchase a variety of kites or make your own, and drive to the nearest open field to fly it. The caress of the wind will help you loosen your white-knuckle hold on life and allow you to celebrate that you are alive!

DRIVE YOURSELF TO DISTRACTION!

*Today's interruptions may be God's
appointments in disguise.*

CAROL KENT

ave you ever been forced to take a detour on a trip and then found yourself on a more scenic route? When that happened to me, I discovered that what appeared to be a frustrating deviation from my final destination, turned out to be a much more pleasant journey with less traffic, fewer stoplights, and a more picturesque view. It became an unexpected vacation—but because of my annoyance, I nearly missed it.

Often we are forced to take *alternative routes* in our everyday lives. These deviations from our original course of action may seem like disruptions, but could it be detours are opportunities purposely placed in our pathway? Is it possible that our interruptions are God's appointments and we do not recognize them? When a friend cancels a lunch date, it may be a gift of quiet time alone. Snow days may be opportunities to spend time with the kids, playing games and being a kid again, too. When you have to wait at an appointment, see it as a chance to calm down and perhaps catch up on some reading. Sometimes, when I'm at my dentist's office and looking forward to a few minutes with a *Better Homes and Gardens*, they call me in right away. Now, *that's* frustrating!

A distraction could be exactly what you need when you are at your wit's end. Instead of relying on detours to happen randomly, seek out and plan your own. If you have been involved in a tedious, mind-numbing task, pick a diversion that is exciting and out of the ordinary. When you're feeling exhausted, choose something relaxing. If you've been looking after matters that are serious and intense, find a detour that is fun and frivolous. By doing the opposite, you'll see things from a fresh perspective when you return to your original route. Jigsaw puzzles are great diversions. Leave one out and work on it 5 minutes each day. Being fully immersed and oblivious to external influences is the secret to an effective distraction. Do a crossword puzzle, work on a craft project, or put some photos in a small album. Any leisure activity, hobby, or pastime will work wonders.

Sometimes it's more beneficial to get outdoors. Get in the car and go for a drive, even if it's just to get a cup of flavored coffee, pick up a newspaper or magazine at the drugstore, or buy a piece of fruit at the market. That's "driving yourself to distraction!" The change of scenery will do you good. Let everyone know when you'll be available again. Then, let go of all your worries and cares, and revel in the experience!

DILLYDALLY & DAWDLE

There are a lot of activity addicts who'd love to stop running…if only they knew how.

CHUCK SWINDOLL

awdling is something we'd prefer not to be caught doing. In fact, most of us would rather die than be seen dilly-dallying. It sounds like such a waste of precious time. Dawdling is something our children do that holds us back and throws us off schedule. It's those times when you're ready to jump in the car to run errands, planning to make at least a hundred (and perhaps even a hundred and one) stops over the next 45 minutes, but the kids have other plans. They are intent on following the path of an ant carrying a dead ant, or silently sneaking up on a squirrel to get as close as possible before the little critter realizes what's happening and scurries up a tree. Kids have different priorities.

To dawdle really means to linger, pause, stay behind, hesitate, and delay leaving. When our children do it, we see it as plodding, traipsing, trudging, and impeding us from accomplishing our mission. Try dawdling for a bit today and see how you like it. Take a few moments to pause. Take a breather and linger over a second cup of coffee with a friend or a conversation you're having with your child. Slow down. Move at your own pace. Know what your own pace is, become comfortable with it, and trust it.

Why is it that we are always in some type of whirlwind? Who decided that our lives should resemble a movie on fast-forward? Some of you are moving so quickly that if there was a speed limit on how fast you could go, you'd always be breaking it. A while back, I read an article about "hurry sickness." Ironically, I was in too much of a hurry to read the whole thing. But one suggestion was to think about ways you can train yourself to walk, talk, and eat more slowly. To slow myself down, I've taken up the lost art of strolling, which is not the same as walking. While I love to walk and do it any chance I get, my motive with walking is to get in shape and stay fit. Strolling is different. It's a slow-paced saunter that allows me to meander, pause, reflect, and explore—things I don't do when I'm on a fitness mission. Even saying the word "stroll" is soothing to me. It's a word from a bygone era, and something our grandparents did after dinner. Try it sometime—take a leisurely ramble with an unhurried stride.

Cliff called to me the other morning to come and see something out the front window. He wouldn't tell me what it was but said that if I didn't come right away, I'd miss it and then I'd be sorry. There was such urgency in his voice that I knew I'd better go. I remember I was in the middle of something, because I'm always in the middle of something, and didn't appreciate the interruption. I also knew if I didn't get there in time, he would never let me forget what I had missed. Because of his insistence, I couldn't begin to imagine what it might be. Was an airplane landing in our yard? A herd of disoriented moose that had made their way down from the north and were now trampling our garden? Could it be the new neighbors across the street were dancing naked on their front lawn? As I made my way and stood by his side, I saw it—a hummingbird hovering just outside the window. Cliff was in awe of its exquisite beauty and the fact that a bit of God's splendor had stopped by to visit us this morning. As I watched, I was in awe too, but more in admiration of my husband than the hummingbird. In his own special way, he has gradually been teaching me to slow down, to dillydally, to dawdle a bit, and linger a while. Now, when I forgo whatever I'm working on to ride along with him to the hardware store, I don't see it as loafing. In fact, I find myself on the lookout for hummingbirds these days!

5-MINUTE ENERGIZERS

When I'm feeling blue,
I start breathing again!

hen you're closer to the end of your rope than the end of your to-do list, and you barely have enough time or energy to read this book, you need some quick pick-me-up techniques. You might think you don't have time to squeeze in some R and R or a few pampering pleasures, but if you will give yourself permission to nurture yourself, you'll get the boost you need to keep going. Even you have enough time for these simple, easy-to-implement energizers.

Start by plotting out several time slots each week for MTO—"Mom's Time Out." Put a magnet calendar on the refrigerator and write MTO opposite the open time slots. Explain to your family that this is your quiet time and that you need to be by yourself for 5 minutes.

Get outside and focus on the greenery around you—grass, trees, potted plants, shrubs. Whether you're in your backyard, on a balcony, or at a nearby park, being close to living things in a natural setting is like breathing in a tonic for the soul. When you can manage to get away, visit a local greenhouse, florist shop, or garden center. Buy a few flowering plants and set aside a windowsill or special spot for them. Remind yourself as you tend and care for them, you are also nurturing yourself.

Water is an energizer, too. If you can't manage a full soak in the tub, try massaging your hands under warm, running water for 3 or 4 minutes. Use a citrus scented soap—tangerine, grapefruit, or orange—to invigorate. Choose lavender, chamomile, or jasmine for a calming effect. Rinse thoroughly and dry off briskly with a fluffy towel. Finish off by applying some luxurious hand cream, in a coordinating scent, if possible. Massage your hands by rubbing each finger individually and then pressing the thumb of one hand in a gentle circular motion around the palm of the other hand. You'll feel the stress being released as you do.

Sit in a chair and do some gentle head rolls and neck stretches. Try some shoulder scrunches by bringing them up toward your ears, and back down as far as you can, then up and down again a few times. Roll your shoulders in a circular motion, first forward, then backward. Finish off with some deep breathing or a time of total relaxation.

When you need an instant boost, do the energy shake. Stretch your arms out in front of you and make a fist. Release your fingers, stretch them, then make a fist, and release again. Now, shake your hands vigorously as if they were wet and you're trying to dry them off. Combine it with a few minutes of jogging on the spot several times a day, and you'll feel as though you've had a spring tonic!

A 5-minute energizer for you might be playing with the new puppy, reading a magazine or one page of a novel, having the kids brush and play with your hair, swinging on the swing in the backyard, listening to music or a book on tape, or watching the sunrise or sunset. Whatever it is, remind yourself that moms who nurture their souls are more patient, less resentful, and don't get sick as often. You're doing everyone a favor!

LUNCH DATES
OVER THE PHONE

Without fellowship, life is not worth living.

LAURIE COLWIN

hen you become a mother, you may need friends more than ever—for support, encouragement, and external input—but you also have less time for them. That's the unfortunate reality. So when you're longing for some adult conversation with a good friend yet can't manage to get together, try arranging to have lunch, coffee, or tea over the phone.

Simply call ahead to determine a good time for both of you for your phone date, and agree that during this call it's permissible to eat while you are talking. Treat this date as seriously as any other appointment, no matter how tempted you may be to cancel when other priorities tend to crop up. When the day arrives, call your friend and each of you can settle in with a cup of hot tea and a salad, or a bowl of soup and a sandwich, or coffee and a muffin, for a good long chat.

Naturally I'd rather visit with my family or friends in person, but let's face it—sometimes getting together just isn't possible because of timing or distance. While it is more gratifying to be able to have a "real" visit, it isn't always an option and preserving friendships over the phone is better than not visiting at all.

Vary your phone date to suit your schedule. You may prefer to arrange to have your morning coffee or afternoon tea together.

Another idea is one I got from my daughters who both lead jam-packed, multifaceted lives as moms, homemakers, and full-time college students. They choose a time when they can call each other on their cordless phones, and while chatting, they get some routine daily chores out of the way. Both girls agree it takes the drudgery out of simple tasks such as dusting, folding laundry, putting clothes away, emptying the dishwasher, tidying, or cleaning out a junk drawer. Chores become more pleasant, and they seem to get them done much quicker while enjoying their visit on the phone.

These are times you'll want to socialize with your friends without the children around. To occupy little ones during your phone lunch date, make them their own little sack lunches (peanut butter and banana sandwiches on crusty bread, carrot and celery sticks with dip, apple slices, oatmeal cookies, a can of fruit juice) to take outdoors in summertime, or in cooler climates, let them "camp out" in a makeshift indoor tent—a blanket or quilt draped over two chairs with plastic underneath.

Is there someone you've been longing to visit or get to know but it's simply out of the question? It's incredible what you can learn about a woman you've seen at the playground every day for over a year in just one phone conversation! Why not plan to have morning coffee, afternoon tea, or a luncheon over the phone? You'll be glad you took the time to make a new friend.

IN YOUR DREAMS!

Put your ear down next to your
soul and listen hard.

<small>ANNE SEXTON</small>

o you have a dream? Could you describe what you'd like to see taking place in your life that may not be happening right now? Most of us would not have a problem rhyming off what we *don't* want, but we're not exactly sure when it comes to what we do want. At least, we've never expressed it, or if you're like most moms, you've never really given it much thought.

You might know what you want for your children's lives and futures, or you may be aware of your husband's goals and plans. But let me ask you this: If you could do, be, or have anything in this world, and you knew you could not fail, what would you dare to dream? If you could create your ideal life, what would it look like? Try to quiet your mind and visualize it: *Where would you live? What would your ideal home look like? How much spare time would you have, and how would you spend it? What would you do to stay healthy and fit? What kind of car would you drive, how would you dress, and where would you vacation? Would you have flower gardens, a sunroom, or a gazebo?*

Describe your relationships with your husband, with your children, other family members, friends, God. In your dream life, what would your children be doing? (Silly question. Of course, they'd be cleaning their rooms before they get condemned by the Board of Health, using soap when they wash up, wearing clean socks, eating broccoli, chewing with their mouths shut, using manners, replacing the toilet paper, feeding the dog, turning off the computer games to practice their musical instruments, asking if you need help bringing in the groceries, and using an actual handkerchief instead of their sleeve!) Seriously, changes *can* happen as a result of dreaming. What you think about and envision has a powerful effect on what will happen in your life. After all, everything that was ever created started in someone's thoughts.

To ignite your dreams and stimulate your imagination, create a dream collage. Get yourself a piece of poster board, a pair of scissors, and a glue stick. Flip through an assortment of magazines, brochures, catalogs, and travel guidebooks. Clip the ones you find appealing or relate to your dreams—images that symbolize comfort and relaxation, health and energy, an exotic vacation spot, new living room furniture, or a fun-filled evening with your family. You can also use photocopies of photographs, old greeting cards, postcards, and keepsakes from happy times—theatre tickets, concert programs, vacation pictures. If you can't find a certain image to attach to a dream, try sketching it yourself. Put yourself in the dream, too, by cutting out photographs of you and attaching them to the appropriate images—a woman who is physically fit, a couple relaxing together in a hammock under a shade tree, or a mom reading to her child. Play with all your images on the poster board, moving them around until a pattern evolves. Then, glue your collage in place and put it where you can see it regularly. Pictures help to keep the dream alive. They strengthen our resolve. We usually say, "I'll believe it when I see it." The truth is, we're more likely to see it once we can believe it! So go ahead and believe—in your dreams!

FULFILL A DREAM

I dwell in possibility.

EMILY DICKINSON

s there some part of your life you'd like to transform? Would you like some extra space and time for yourself? Do you feel the need to escape your current circumstances? If you sometimes entertain thoughts of packing up a few belongings, getting a one-way ticket to anywhere, and leaving no forwarding address, maybe what you're lacking is a dream. When you allow yourself to dream and set a goal for yourself, you are *dwelling in possibility*. If you want to stop worrying, lose those 10 pounds of baby fat, spend more time enjoying your family, find a way to catch up on your sleep, have a weekend vacation or pampering spa evening, or enjoy a family meal together, you can attain those dreams through goal-setting. Here are some basic steps and guidelines to help you follow through and achieve your goals.

Start by noticing any disharmony in your life. What is out of balance? Are you experiencing health concerns or conflicts in your relationships? Is there scarcity of finances, time, affection, love, passion, stillness, peace? Do you crave more "alone" time, or perhaps an afternoon out with friends? Maybe you'd simply like to enjoy a single unstructured, unplanned day, or you're missing that carefree, spontaneous, happy-go-lucky person you used to be. One powerful truth about living your dreams is that you'll never leave where you are until you decide where you'd rather be.

Ask yourself these critical questions and write your answers in a journal you've designated for goal setting: *How can I slow down? How can I create more satisfying relationships? What would it take to experience more creativity each day or increase my energy with healthy solutions? How can I feel more joy today?* Next, say to yourself, *I am where I am today because of my past choices. Right now, I am a sum total of all the decisions I have made in my life. If I chose where I am today, I can change my life by changing my choices.*

There is one, and only one, thing God has given each of us absolute control over and that is our power to choose. You choose what you think about, focus and dwell upon, how you spend your time, the people you associate with, even how long you'll talk on the telephone. We say, "I just couldn't get off the phone," but we know there are ways to do it if we get creative enough. Your choices determine all your outcomes. When you start taking responsibility for your choices, you put an end to blaming and complaining. Blamers see themselves as "victims" of their circumstances, and they are powerless to make changes. By accepting responsibility, you take back the key to your happiness, and you unlock the power to change things.

Try doing something—anything—different. When you handle your same old issues with the same old methods, you won't see changes. Albert Einstein told us that doing the same things again and again while expecting different results is a good definition of insanity! To experience new outcomes, change your thoughts. The book of Proverbs tells us, "As a man thinks in his heart, so is he." When you change your thoughts, you change your world.

Picture yourself achieving what it is you'd like to accomplish. If your goal is to be in good physical condition, envision yourself practicing healthy habits—eating nourishing foods, walking outdoors, moving more, and thinking wholesome thoughts. If what you'd like is to have more "me" time, see yourself being still and alone, relaxing, reading quietly, soaking in a tub, snoozing, going for a stroll. Envision yourself spending time with good, confiding friends and building a support team of other moms who understand the challenges you face, so you can offer each other encouragement.

By holding these images in your mind, you'll be more likely to act on them. Good dreams and goals are similar to good principles. They are an effective starting point, but if you don't follow through, you won't get results. Begin by being grateful for what you already have. In all your dreaming, all your goal setting, and all your planning, remember that the only thing you have for sure is today. Shift your attention to what is good, what you can be thankful for, and what is right about your life.

PART 2

MOMS NEED PAMPERING, TOO

TIME TO ESCAPE

*You know you're a mom when you hire
a sitter because you haven't been out with your
husband in ages, then spend half the night
checking in on the kids.*

o you ever feel as though the best way to improve your life would be to leave town, change your name, and start all over again? I know I have. Over the years of being a mom, I've had numerous secret fantasies about dying my hair, getting all new ID, and beginning a fresh life someplace else. If you have never thought about doing this, you are to be applauded for your capacity to endure. If you *have* contemplated doing this, you are like most of us. Take solace in knowing you are not alone. If all the moms who ever thought about leaving home actually did something about it, very few of us would be living where we are now! And I find that strangely comforting somehow.

When you are starting to suspect that there may be more to life than *Winnie the Pooh* and *Sesame Street*, and you have an inkling that some conversations may actually go beyond "Please use your indoor voice," "Don't forget to flush," and "Have you ever thought of using soap?," think about planning your escape (for a day, at least). When I was a little girl, my mom sometimes watched a television program called, "Queen for a Day." The lucky winner would get to be pampered and fussed over for one full day, and I think she even got money to go shopping to buy whatever she wanted. (There's a novel idea!) Try to think of yourself as queen for just one day. Get yourself one of those cute, little sparkling tiaras if you think it might help set the mood. And then start planning your escape. Whether the kids are at school or in day care, with their dad or grandparents, or you've traded with another mom, you need to know the little tykes are well-looked after. Then, you can fully enter into this experience with total abandon and won't be spending valuable energy calling home every hour to check up!

A time to escape is a day for leaving routines and schedules behind. It's a day to "just be," to take a miniature vacation or to do nothing. Start by sitting in a cozy, quiet spot with your journal and a pen, get comfortable, and ask yourself, "If I could be queen for one full day, and do anything I wanted, without having to consider the wants and needs of others, what would it be?" This may take a little getting used to if you've never done it. You're bound to have thoughts like, "That could never happen, so why bother considering it." For now, this is merely a fantasy, so go wild! Don't let anything inhibit your imagination. Instead, expand your horizons. Widen your perspective and think in terms of possibilities.

Look over what you've written and determine which aspects could realistically be integrated into your "escape" day. Ponder your passions, consider what would add delight to your life, and make a list. You might include something as simple as packing a nice picnic for yourself. Or, you may choose something more decadent such as going to the theater to see a live play. Have lunch in a restaurant you've never visited—try Japanese or Thai, for example—and then go to the movies.

Consider playing "tourist at home." Visit some spots in your own city or choose a nearby town and go exploring from a tourist's point of view. Meander through a charming boutique. Have coffee at an outdoor café or an old-fashioned ice cream sundae on the porch of a country inn. Browse in a bookstore and stock up on a few titles to tuck away for your next day off. Pick up a postcard to send to a friend. Visit a historical museum or a gallery that features the work of local artists. Take your camera and capture some unique angles of familiar sites. Chat with the "real" tourists. Enjoy a bit of local culture and it may change the way you see your town from now on.

Whether you play for free by attending an outdoor art exhibit or a concert in the park, or invest in a European body wrap at a spa, do whatever seems most frivolous and totally self-indulgent. Luxuriate in your special day…and wear your tiara home!

GO UNDERCOVER

*There's no fun in doing nothing when
you have nothing to do.*

JEROME K. JEROME

he best time to go *undercover*, to hide out from the world, is when there's too much to do. When you are trying to function on overload, you're most vulnerable to mishaps and mistakes, and most in need of some of the gentle, tender nurturing you lavish so naturally on others. We promise ourselves that once everything's caught up and we have *leftover* time, we'll take a day off to hide out under the covers and play hooky. Here's a news flash for you: There isn't going to be leftover time! You have to snatch it when you need it. The truth is you'll get much more out of playing hooky when you're not all caught up. You'll come back uplifted, energized, and inspired with a fresh enthusiasm for all you left behind.

But then there's the guilt thing. It seems moms can't win. We always have to feel guilty about something. Mothers who stay at home hear, "What do you *do* all day?" Working moms hear, "Who's looking after your children while you're at work?" When you play hooky for a day, your inner critic does the job for you: *Just look what happens when you take time out to nurture yourself! You lie around all afternoon watching Oprah and polishing off a pint of chocolate chip ice cream and a whole bag of gingersnaps. The beds don't get made, there's nothing for supper, and the laundry is piling up. While everyone else in the world is getting their life in order, you're goofing off!*

What would you say to a friend who was living a life like yours and needed to escape? You'd probably remind her that she'd be better off with a little time out. It doesn't necessarily have to be a full day. Taking a couple of hours on a Saturday afternoon, leaving work early on a Friday, or staying home from the meeting you didn't want to attend anyway to watch *Masterpiece Theater* would suffice. Do whatever it takes to go undercover. Call in and use up a mental-health day, hire a sitter, take the kids to day care, or exchange "hooky days" with another mom. Maybe you could offer to trade services instead. Think of a talent you have for something she doesn't enjoy. Offer to help with wallpapering her bedroom, stenciling a border, mending kids' clothes, sewing curtains, or baking the dessert she needs for her next family gathering in exchange for watching your kids.

Once you find a way to be alone, ask yourself what you yearn for that would bring you peace and contentment. Whatever it is, the key word when playing hooky is *play*. Set aside your regular routines and luxuriate in idleness. Lollygag and laze about. Don't wear a watch, answer the phone, or check your E-mail. Do only what you find comforting. When the day is over, pick up the kids, serve take-out for supper, put on some cozy pajamas, and turn in early.

THE 5-MINUTE ROYAL TREATMENT

*The soul has an absolute, unforgiving need for
regular excursions into enchantment.
It requires them like the body
needs food and the mind needs thought.*

THOMAS MOORE

hen a little girl was having a difficult time grasping the concept of marriage, her father got out the wedding album in an attempt to help her. Once he explained the wedding ceremony, the little girl said, "Oh, now I see! That's when Mommy came to work for us."

It's not hard to see why that little girl—or our children—might think that's true. A while ago, when I seriously scrutinized my "to-do" list, I noticed something dreadfully wrong. It wasn't so much what was *on* the list—buy a present for the baby shower, organize the hall closet, call the members of my volunteer committee, bake a dessert for the church supper, pick up kitty litter. The problem was what was *missing* from my list...time for me, for excursions into enchantment. Now that may sound a bit selfish, but think about it. As moms, we spend most of our time taking care of others—our children, spouses, elderly parents, friends, Sunday school students, and coworkers—but we spend next to no time making sure we're as balanced and cared for as all the other people in our lives.

On the brink of burnout, I knew I had to make some changes. While I was sure a 10-day trip to the Mediterranean would solve the problem, I decided to settle for a few simpler—and more budget-friendly—pampering rituals. Here are some ways to experience the simple pleasures and sweet indulgences that will make sure your children don't think your wedding was the day you were hired to work for them!

Plan a temporary escape. Do you remember snow days? During bleak winters, it was always a treat to be able to stay in our pajamas, sip hot chocolate by the fire, munch on popcorn, and watch movies or play Monopoly. Even without the snow, plan to do that again for part of a day. For another escape, go to your local coffee shop one evening or when the kids are in school, order a special blend, and read a few chapters of that book you've been longing to get into. Allow yourself some private time each day, even if it's only 5 minutes at a time.

Splurge on one thing just for you. Buy a bouquet of spring flowers for yourself at the market. Indulge in an expensive brand of ice cream, or gourmet hot chocolate and a pretty china mug. Pick up a bottle of your favorite perfume, a new CD, or some lacy silk lingerie, even if no one else will see you in it! Each time you wear, smell, eat, or drink whatever you bought, it will brighten your day and remind you that you are special.

Reward yourself when you've achieved a goal. Sink into your tub for a long luxurious soak with bubbles and candlelight. Snuggle up in bed with a good book. Go for a leisurely stroll. Put on your favorite music, turn it up loud, and dance. This time is not about being selfish. It's about recognizing you are a precious woman created by God, and you deserve to be treated as such. Put yourself on the to-do list and take an excursion into enchantment!

A NURTURING SPA DAY

If it weren't for stress,
I'd have no energy at all.

f you need an energy boost but have never contemplated spending a day at a spa because you thought it was too time-consuming or a luxury you could never afford, start by doing a little investigating. You may be pleasantly surprised, and besides, it doesn't cost anything to inquire—or to dream! Make some initial phone calls to local spas and begin gathering information. Take notes and keep them in a personal journal, on a pretty notepad, or in a file folder in your favorite color. That way, once you've decided to invest in yourself with some healthy self-care and pampering, you have all the necessary facts.

Arrange to visit a spa or two in your area to price treatments, pick up brochures, and perhaps even have a private tour of the facilities. Let them know you are new at this and ask all the questions you want about the services available. The staff will be glad to fill you in on all the details. After all, it's their job to make you feel welcome, at ease, and stress-free—and they're good at it. (If they're not willing, leave and go somewhere else—quickly!)

When you get back home, or later in the evening before bed, change into something comfy, curl up with a cup of tea, and review the materials you've collected. In a journal, write out when you'd like to have a spa day, whether you prefer a weekday or weekend, and whether you'll go alone, or with your husband, or a friend. Ask yourself how many services you would like to indulge in, which treatments you would choose, and how often you'd like to visit a spa. Don't even consider budget or time constraints at this point. This exercise is just to get you dreaming—and that doesn't cost a thing or take much time. From the brochures, clip the pictures, images, and words that make you feel calm, relaxed, peaceful, and carefree, and glue them into your journal. Go through women's magazines or travel brochures, too, and seek out pictures that represent pampering and nurturing activities. Next, start a special savings account (or assign a standard envelope), decide how much you will put away regularly toward your pampering treatments, and look forward to booking your first appointment.

Once you're ready, the indulgences available are limitless. They range from full-body aromatherapy and relaxation massages to revitalizing hair and scalp treatments; manicures and pedicures; herbal facials; nourishing body wraps; and mud baths. Get ready to drift off into dreamland while someone fusses over you for a change.

Aside from visiting a spa, take advantage of department store specials that offer free cosmetic makeovers and skin care consultations, or pay your hair stylist a few extra dollars to massage your scalp before your regular shampoo.

When someone wants to buy you a present—Mother's Day, Valentine's Day, your birthday—ask for gift certificates for hair treatments, spa services, or skin care products. Start investing in your health and wellness. Make it a priority to nurture yourself—body, mind, and soul.

A SPA
AT HOME

*You know you're a mom if you only manage
to shave one leg per day!*

magine what it would be like to actually luxuriate at home with your own pampering spa retreat! With a little planning and imagination, it can be done. You may even get to shave both legs in the same session! While you might be a mom who does retreat to the bathtub regularly when you have the need to escape, there's more than one way to take a bath. Try integrating a complete spa experience into your regular bubble bath.

Arrange to have the children occupied—with dad, grandma, your sister, or a good friend. Consider exchanging "spa time" with another mom. You might suggest that you'll have her children for a sleepover while she pampers herself, and she can do the same for you when it's your turn. When you're all ready, lock the door and prepare your bathroom for an unforgettable bathing ritual you'll want to retreat to as often as possible. Strategically place a few scented candles around the room so that their flickering flame shimmers against a wall or reflects in the water. Put a plant or vase of fresh flowers nearby. Place an inflatable terry cloth-covered bath pillow and bath tray in the tub, and run the water. Gather your bath products and other accessories and place them nearby: essential oils for relaxation and aromatherapy, bath and shower gels, scented bath salts or bubbles, a long-necked back brush, a loofah sponge, a pumice stone and exfoliating cream, and the best part—a box of chocolates! Have a pair of silk pajamas or a terry-cloth robe and slippers nearby, and some fluffy cotton towels that have been warmed in the dryer. Put your hair up in a pretty ribbon or scarf, and apply a facial mask. Add some soothing classical background music and a steamy cup of herbal tea or fruit-flavored sparkling mineral water, and you're ready to soak away your cares. Turn the lights down low, or replace regular bulbs with soft pink ones for a calming ambience.

Slowly step into your tub full of sparkling warm water, sweetened with soothing oils or scented salts. Lay your head back and enjoy the tranquility, or read from a magazine or good book, but nothing too deep. Relax and let the water wash over you. Notice how buoyant your limbs are. Bask in the candlelight. Play with the water. Stay as long as you need to wash away all your stress. When you're ready to emerge, wrap yourself in a warm towel and dry off. Lather your entire body with rich moisturizing body lotion. Use a pumice stone on your tootsies and massage in some soothing peppermint cream. Finish off by applying your signature perfume and talcum powder. Now is a good time to have a manicure and pedicure. Don't forget to apply some pretty polish.

It can be costly to have a good supply of bath and body products on hand for your special spa treatments. For special occasions, when people want to buy you gifts, ask for your favorite lotions, perfume, soap, talc, bubble bath, and shower gel. It makes shopping easy for them, and you'll have everything you need for your next pampering spa day. There are some bath recipes you can mix up at home. Make a simple facial mask by blending oatmeal and honey. For a beautiful bath sachet, mix oatmeal, salt, essential oils, and fragrant herbs such as lavender, rose petals, or rosemary. Tie it in a cotton bag and hang under the running water as the tub fills. Of all essential oils to choose from, lavender is probably the most versatile and helpful for stress control, tension relief, and general body aches and pains. After hearing about a soothing and revitalizing hair and scalp treatment using olive oil with a few drops of lavender, I decided to try it at home one evening. I applied the mixture, wrapped my head in plastic wrap, and covered it with a warm towel. Afterward, I sham-pooed several times to be sure to get all the oil out. When I crawled into bed with my husband that night, I asked him if I smelled like olive oil. "No," he replied. "Why, do I smell like Popeye?"

Whether you blend your products at home or purchase them, whether you lay back in the tub and close your eyes or choose to read, whether you enjoy candlelight or prefer to bathe in complete darkness, this is your time to be nurtured. Take time to care for yourself. If you don't, then who will?

INDULGE IN A MASSAGE

If I'd known I was gonna live this long,
I'd have taken better care of myself.

EUBIE BLAKE

s a mom, so much of your day is spent nurturing and caring for others. So the mere thought of someone nurturing you for a change probably sounds tantalizing. Having a massage goes beyond merely wanting someone to pamper you. It's about fortifying yourself and building up your resources so you can stay healthy and continue caring for those you love. Synonyms for the word *nurture* are *nourish, strengthen, sustain, support,* and *keep alive!* And if you're not kept alive, you know what the alternative is! So, in that case, remind yourself that a massage is a sort of rescue mission, saving you from harm and possible death! (Telling yourself this will make it a whole lot easier to indulge without the guilt. Telling others this is a way of gaining their support.)

The word *nourish* comes from the Latin, *nutrire,* meaning to breastfeed, which also gives us the words *nutrition* and *nurse.* Maybe it's time for us to be nurse to ourselves. A full-body massage is one way to do that. It is the utmost in self-care because it benefits your whole person—physically, mentally, emotionally, and spiritually. It can soothe or stimulate your muscles, nervous system, cells, tissues, and glands. Studies show that a good massage can help to balance your digestion and metabolism. If you are feeling off-kilter, massage is one way to restore harmony. If you're pregnant, some massage tables have stretch material in the midsection (just like you do!), allowing you to lie on your tummy while the therapist massages your aching back. Imagine feeling physically good in spite of the fact that your body is larger than a small car and your energy is at an all-time low!

When I first started having massages on a regular basis, the tears would flow freely. I wasn't exactly sure why, but I couldn't seem to stop the crying. I discovered that muscles store memory, as well as all the tension we experience in a day, or a lifetime. It's no wonder that, when emotions are being released, they have to find an outlet. After that, I didn't attempt to hold the tears back. They were cathartic and cleansing. Eventually, my mood fluctuations seemed to even out, and I was enjoying my life more than I had ever imagined possible.

For that hour you are on the table, you can shut out the world and relax in a heavenly sanctuary. To benefit the most, have a long soak in the tub before you go. Once you're on the table, wrapped in a warm thermo-blanket (regardless of our age, we all like to be "tucked in"), immerse yourself in the atmosphere. Delight in the flicker of candlelight and soothing background music with sounds of ocean waves lapping the shore. Close your eyes and soak up the experience. A full-body relaxation massage can make you feel like a new woman.

SELF-MASSAGE
BASICS

Happiness is an unexpected foot rub.

or those times when you simply want to relax at home, aren't able to get away from the family, or if your budget won't allow for a professional treatment, there are still ways you can benefit from a massage. Take 5 minutes to give yourself a mini-massage right at home. After a bath, before you fall into bed at night, or anytime during the day when you are feeling tense and tight, get out some massage oil and have a quick, relaxing treatment.

For an at-home face massage, apply a little oil or cream to your hands and rub them together until they are warm with friction. Place both palms on your face and use your fingertips to massage the warmth into your skin. Begin on your forehead and slide down over your cheekbones and all the way to your throat. Rub your hands again and press the "heel," or the pads of your fingers, over tired eyes and gently press around the eye muscles for a few moments. Follow with a hand and finger massage since they're already coated with oil.

Tap your scalp lightly but vigorously with all your fingers for several minutes, working from the crown of your head, down the sides of your face, around your ears, and the back of your neck. To release a stiff neck and tender shoulders, roll a tennis ball between your back and the sofa or floor. Or, use the wall and move the ball around by bending and straightening your knees. Most department stores sell small, hand-held wooden massagers with rollers you can use to run up and down your arms and legs or across your shoulders. For a foot massage, roll your tootsies in a basin filled with marbles. When my children were young, two of us would lie on the bed or the floor beside each other "end to end," and simultaneously massage each other's feet!

You may want to add the benefits of aromatherapy to your massage oil. You can purchase aromatic oils or make your own. Start with a base such as almond, sunflower, or olive oil, and add an essential oil to it. Choose the scent depending on your need at the time. Some of these highly concentrated essential oils soothe, relax, and calm, while others stimulate, energize, and rejuvenate. If you are worn out or just plain exhausted, try chamomile. It relaxes muscle tension, soothes nerves, and calms your mind. Lemon improves poor circulation, stimulates metabolism, and invigorates your senses. Lavender, which is probably the most versatile of all essential oils, can be used for treating many stress conditions including nervous tension and the monthly crazies that go along with PMS. For headaches, simply massage your temples with a drop of lavender.

Even children benefit from massage. We know that with newborns, touch can mean the difference between life and death. The instinctive cuddling between mother and infant forms an amazing bond. Studies show that toddlers who get daily 5-minute rubdowns are more responsive and sleep better at night. An at-home massage is a 5-minute retreat that can benefit the entire family!

READING RETREATS

Of all the diversions of life, there is none so proper to fill up its empty spaces as the reading of useful and entertaining authors.

JOSEPH ADDISON

We live in an era where many of the old diversions of life have become a lost art. Reading, especially, is fast becoming an endangered pleasure. Video and computer games, and other forms of electronic entertainment, are slowly replacing former pastimes. Storytelling and poetry reading are also vanishing, even though we can be deeply touched by hearing a human voice narrating a lovely poem, reading a Scripture verse, or reciting a meaningful quote. Interestingly, it can be just as stirring to read aloud to yourself. Speaking and hearing the words somehow helps us to comprehend them on a whole new level. Take a moment by yourself to read or recite something out loud. It can be a favorite story, poem, or meaningful verse. Allow yourself to articulate each word vividly and experience the new form it takes as you make it your own. The next time you read a much-loved storybook to your child, place a tape recorder nearby. Do all the voices and use lots of expression. Later, your child can enjoy the comforts of listening to your voice even if you're not available, or if you are relaxing with a 5-minute reading retreat of your own. If he has the book and can read along at the same time, it will also enrich his reading skills.

Most of us know where a good bookstore or library is located. We might pass one regularly as we rush from the bank to the grocery store, from the school to the office. Perhaps we even promise ourselves that we'll stop in one of these days—when life slows down a little and we have a moment to pick up a good book. Months go by, however, and one of these days never comes. We miss so much when that happens! Books can open up a whole new world, expanding our everyday existence in ways we cannot imagine. They take us on travels, introduce us to interesting people, and teach us about new things. They enrich our lives.

One day soon, plan a retreat for yourself in a bookstore or library. Allow yourself time to browse: don't rush your visit. Enjoy the scent and grain of the books. Go ahead and read a few bits and pieces. Don't be surprised when something interesting whets your reading appetite. When was the last time you enjoyed a captivating novel? At one time, I considered reading fiction to be a waste of time and always opted for books dealing with personal growth and self-discovery. Then I found, when carefully chosen, some novels encouraged, relaxed, and refreshed me, while others caused me to stretch, or exposed me to people and places I might not otherwise experience. When you need a total escape, retreat with an absorbing piece of fiction. Ask friends for recommendations or simply go and browse, reading the first few pages before making your selection. Allow yourself to become immersed in the story, and be on the lookout for lessons to be discovered.

It's fun to read children's literature, too. What were your favorite classics from childhood? Perhaps you enjoyed Kenneth Grahame's *The Wind in the Willows* or *Anne of Green Gables* by L.M. Montgomery. Experience all over again the expectancy, enchantment, and simplicity these books brought to you. Visit the children's section of the library and seek out *Charlotte's Web* by E.B. White or go to a bookstore and pick up a fresh copy of *The Secret Garden* or *Little Women*. When your child sees you reading and enjoying a good book, she or he may want to identify with you. Keep a reading basket with a journal, pens, and hi-liters by your favorite chair. With everything handy, you may be tempted to read more often, even if you only have a few minutes. Lend your books to others and tape a lined sheet inside the back cover that says: This book has been enjoyed by…and have readers sign it. What a great way to record, for yourself and others, all those who have shared in the joy of your personal collection. Surround yourself with books and build your personal library. I can relate to Marcus T. Cicero when he declared, "A room without books is like a body without a soul."

ENERGIZE
YOUR LIFE

*I'm so tired that the only way I can brush
my teeth is by laying the toothbrush on the counter
and moving my mouth back and forth over it.*

racticing 5-minute retreats is about stress-proofing with simple indulgences and innocent pleasures that add delight to your life. It's also about building up your reserves of energy so that you can stay calm during the storms of life—handling the ups and downs of being a mom with peace and harmony. Mostly, it's about taking better care of you. One of the practical ways you can do that is to maximize your energy through the foods you choose to eat.

Your body is an energy system and it functions best with efficient fuel. When you are feeling lethargic and run down, it may be that you're not providing your body with the right type of fuel. If you're not, then you can't expect your body to perform at its maximum level. The nutrients you put into your body every day are affecting your moods, memory, energy levels, sleep patterns, and general health. They also influence your ability to cope with the normal demands of being a mother, including the days when the furnace breaks down, you get stopped for speeding on your way to pick up the kids at basketball practice, and the dog makes a mess on the carpet. Your reaction to these situations has the ability to affect everyone else in the house. Whether you want to be or not, you are the hub of the household wheel and the family is riding on you. That may sound like a lot of pressure, but that's exactly why it's crucial to take the very best care of yourself and make the effort to invest in your health and well-being in every way possible.

When you're stressed out and running on empty all the time, your body uses up the B-vitamins in your system, so they must be replaced. But when you're at your wit's end, do you crave foods that are a good source of B-vitamins, such as brown rice, liver, spinach, tuna, or oatmeal? Probably not. "Behind every successful mom," said cartoonist Stephanie Piro, "is a substantial amount of coffee." If you're like me, you go for coffee and a donut, or cola and a chocolate bar! Not only are these snacks void of B-vitamins, they are filled with caffeine and sugar—the very elements that destroy those nutrients in our body. The first step in reclaiming your energy is to cut back on sugar and caffeine. Because they are both highly addictive, it may take a while to wean yourself from them, especially if these are the foods you have typically chosen during high-stress times.

There is one simple rule I have learned when it comes to increasing your energy: Start adding real food to your diet. In other words, eat food in a form that is closest to its natural state. For instance, you don't see French fries growing on trees, diet soda flowing in the streams, or sugar coated cereal with purple marshmallows growing in a garden. Fields are not full of fast-cooking oats and instant rice. This means you'll want to eat more whole grains and also high-water content foods, meaning fruits and vegetables, preferably fresh and raw. For extra roughage, include those with edible skins. "Until I was 12," says Mollie Katzen, author of *Moosewood Cookbook,* "I thought spaghetti came from a can, and that vegetables grew in the freezer. When I discovered that green beans grew in the ground, I thought it was a miracle."

Most of us think cooking meals that are nourishing will be expensive and take all day to prepare. With our full lives, it seems the best we can do on some days is grab something at a fast-food restaurant or heat up a frozen microwave entrée. These choices are faster but they have little nutritional value and can cost a small fortune. Start to switch your eating habits slowly by adding to your diet steamed vegetables drizzled with olive oil, raw vegetables with a tasty dip, baked potatoes with their skins, a fresh fruit cup for dessert, oatmeal for breakfast, and popcorn, graham crackers, or yogurt for snacks. I am often saddened when I see what goes into some people's shopping carts. Now, I'm not suggesting that I eat perfectly at all times. I've had days when I've been so upset over the squabbling going on at bedtime, the homework that went missing the night before but mysteriously showed up just as the school bus came the next morning, and kids hollering, "Yuck! I'm not eating this!" that I've been forced to consume a half-gallon of butter pecan ice cream. But at least these days, that's the exception to the rule. A mom's gotta do what a mom's gotta do!

PROGRAM PLEASURE
INTO YOUR DAY

*You know you're a mom when you say at least
once a day, "I'm not cut out for
this job," but you know you wouldn't
trade it for anything!*

s I interviewed moms while researching for this book, it
didn't take long to realize how poor most of us are at
providing self-care. The most contented women I met
were those who actively pursue and schedule activities that nourish
the spirit and comfort the soul. For starters, you have to know what
would provide pleasure and make you feel pampered, nurtured, and
relaxed. Get out your journal and start your list. Remember, the
things you do to look after you should not be considered optional
activities.

Set aside time for yourself and celebrate life's simple pleasures.
One way you can do that is to turn routine chores into 5-minute
retreats. Light some candles nearby, play classical music or songs you
can hum along to, and make a cup of herbal tea to sip as you work.
Reward yourself for a job well-done with a treat afterward—visit a
friend or your sister, read a chapter of a good page-turner you've
been longing to get into, or shop for your favorite perfume and
maybe even get the matching lotion!

Plan some activities that will make you feel alive in your body. In
a culture preoccupied with body image, it's wonderful to simply feel
vibrant and healthy. Whether it's dancing alone in your living room
to your favorite music, running on the beach, making snow angels,

walking briskly in the crisp autumn air, or skipping rope on the patio, celebrate that you are alive, full of life, and on the move.

Arrange to have a "de-stress" evening at home. On a cold night, warm your pajamas in the dryer for a few minutes before putting them on. Make a fire in the fireplace, light some candles, pop in a favorite video, have a cup of hot cocoa or apple cider with cinnamon, munch on popcorn, and snuggle in for a night at the movies.

When you tuck the kids in at night, make it a priority to spend an extra few minutes with them. Get right into bed and under the covers for a bedtime chat. Read to them or have them read to you. Say those three little words: "I love you." When you say it to others regularly, watch how often you'll hear it back!

Hands down, one of the best perks about being a mom is spending time with your kids. You know you wouldn't trade it for anything. Whether you're snuggling with your toddler, having a game of Scrabble with your second grader, or playing basketball with your teenager, this is the stuff pure delight is made of.

Life's simple pleasures are priceless. Sometimes it seems as though money is the key to experiencing the best that life has to offer. But money cannot buy joy, delight, tranquility, inner peace, or harmony.

PART 3

BE KIND TO YOURSELF

NOBODY'S PERFECT

*If you were perfect, you'd have very little in
common with the rest of the world!*

ow much of our lives is needlessly squandered away by our irrational determination to achieve perfection? Perhaps we were raised in homes where we were compelled to live up to impossible standards and unrealistic expectations. Maybe it's the false images we are fed daily through the media that tell us: Unless we are perfect in every way, we're missing out on the best life has to offer. In our society, it seems we are reminded repeatedly that unless we have the perfect body, shiniest hair, prettiest fingernails, appropriate number of vacations, right type of car, live in the best neighborhood, and wear the most stylish clothes, we couldn't possibly experience true happiness!

Our culture subliminally feeds us hidden messages that perfection is not only to be desired, it is a worthy goal to strive toward. But recovering perfectionists will tell us, often good enough really is good enough. (Unless you are a brain surgeon about to operate—then I hope you are striving for perfection!) For most of us, it is time to leave the status quo behind and run our own race, not the one the world puts before us. I believe we should strive to attain excellence rather than perfection. Let's leave frivolous, inconsequential, and fruitless endeavors behind. When we do, we'll be making life richer for ourselves and our families.

When I was about 10 years old, my mother taught me to bake. I loved working in the kitchen. Everything about baking captivated me, from measuring and mixing ingredients to getting my hands in the dough, and most of all, the mouth-watering aromas coming from the oven. Cookies, in particular gingersnaps, were my favorite to bake. But each time I made them, I compared the end result with store-bought gingersnaps my friends had in their lunch boxes and was invariably disappointed. When I exclaimed to my mother, "Next time, I'll try harder to make them perfect," she reminded me that the makers of those store-bought cookies were attempting to get theirs to look like the homemade variety! What a waste of time and energy that would have been for me to attempt perfection based on a false perception.

"Perfectionism," says organizational consultant Anne Wilson Schaef, "is self-abuse of the highest order." For 5 minutes today, tackle one activity in which you will consciously aim for excellence rather than perfection. Accept yourself. Accept your spouse. Resign yourself to the way your child makes the bed or sets the table. As Napoleon stated, "The future destiny of a child is always the work of its mother." By encouraging quality in place of flawlessness, you'll be teaching your children a valuable life lesson.

ESCAPE THE COMPARISON TRAP

*Since you are like no other being ever created
since the beginning of time,
you are incomparable.*

Brenda Ueland

ave you ever compared yourself to anyone—your sister, your neighbor, a good friend? I imagine you have, since in all my travels, I've never met a woman who hasn't. We compare all sorts of things, including our physical appearance, body type, education, intellect, talent, career success, financial status, homes, husbands, kids, cars, and material possessions. I have a sign in my office that says, "Comparison equals depression." Whenever we compare ourselves in any way, we are setting ourselves up for possible disappointment, frustration, and unhappiness. Comparison is never fair because we are all unique with different goals, dreams, aspirations, and personal attributes. We are all at various stages in our personal growth. We are each originals—rare and one-of-a-kind.

The biggest problem with comparing ourselves with anyone is that we almost always come out the loser. The reason is that we tend to compare the very worst aspect of our lives with the very best of others. It's no wonder we come away feeling depressed.

All I have to do to feel bad about my own life is pick up a magazine and read an article about "Mrs. Perfect." You've probably read a similar article. This lady is married to a politician; homeschools eight children; sews all their clothes and her own designer fashions; makes her own jams, jellies, and pickles; holds massive dinner parties and prepares all the gourmet dishes herself; paints, wallpapers, and stencils the rooms in her home; shingles the roof in her spare time; and models for *Vogue* because she's six feet tall and ultra slim with Tina Turner legs. She's the one who says on occasion, "Sometimes I forget to eat!" (Oh, come now. I forget my keys, forget to turn off the iron, or forget I have something on the stove, but I don't think I've ever forgotten to eat!)

We beat ourselves up when we think we don't measure up. You are a matchless, exclusive, irreplaceable gem. There is nothing common or ordinary about you. Only you can give your family, your community, your workplace, or the world exactly what you have to offer. No one can fill your role here on this earth. You were created with a purpose, a mission, and only you can accomplish it!

You are a VIP…a very important person. I was sharing this concept at a conference a while ago and I said to the audience in general, "I want you to know you are sitting in the seat of a VIP." Well, I happened to be looking at a girl in the front row at the time, and do you know what she did? She jumped out of her seat and said, "I'm so sorry. I didn't know this seat was taken!" It's sad, but true, many of us don't see ourselves as VIPs either.

It's time to run your own race. My husband, whose hobby is drag racing, tells me when he's going down the track, he doesn't really take into consideration what the competition is doing. Instead, he determines how fast he wants to go, how quickly he wants to get to the end of the track, and then he runs his own race. What the other racer does is not going to influence him one bit. Isn't that good advice for us? You determine what a good life is for you. Go ahead and redefine success and happiness in your own terms. Get out of the comparison trap. Start using the gifts God gave you instead of dwelling on the ones given to someone else!

COMPANY'S
NOT COMING

Treat your family like company
and your company like family.

lthough you may not be having company for dinner, guess who is coming? You and your family! By choosing to dine together rather than merely eat for the sake of ingesting something that is somewhat nutritious, you can turn the dinner table into a safe haven, a refuge from the rest of the world. Treat your family like company and mealtime will become a retreat for you and your loved ones.

Imagine how the scene would unfold if we treated our company the way we often treat family members. We'd greet the guests at the door bellowing, "Where have you been? Dinner was to be at six o'clock and you're late—again! Now get upstairs and wash those grimy hands." Later, we'd scold them for being clumsy and spilling gravy on the tablecloth or dropping crumbs on the floor. We'd nag them about being so picky and insist they try a mouthful of the tofu-lima bean-artichoke-salmon casserole before they decide they don't like it. Don't forget to emphasize the part about starving children in third-world countries, and let them know that packing up their leftovers to ship is not an acceptable option. Finally, remind them they won't be getting their dessert until their plates are clean. While that image may seem comical, we know we would never want our guests to feel uncomfortable in any way.

But what about our families? Now envision the opposite—responding to your children the way you would to company. For one entire week, make an effort to speak to your loved ones as you would your guests and notice the change in their attitudes when it comes to enjoying a meal together.

Preparing a beautifully set and welcoming table plays a big role in making dinner a satisfying experience, yet it is often the last thing we think about if we're not expecting company. For our guests we bring out our finest—the good china, stemmed glassware, cutlery, and our best linens. We light the candles and add a lovely centerpiece of fresh flowers. In contrast, our family mealtimes have become so casual that we're often guilty of gulping down our supper as we hover over the kitchen counter or perch on the edge of a sofa watching television. I'm not suggesting we attempt to serve every meal using starched linens, crystal goblets, and polished silver as my grandmother might have, but there are ways to set an inviting table to make dinnertime an enticing and pleasant event. Start using and enjoying the beautiful items that already fill your cupboards. Don't save their loveliness only for guests. With some candles, a linen tablecloth, and a few fresh flowers, even a modest kitchen table turns a dinner of soup and hot dogs into a feast. Serve macaroni and cheese on the most beautiful dishes you own; use some pretty linen tea towels as place mats or cloth napkins; place a votive candle at each setting; and you will raise the ordinary act of eating into the extraordinary delight of dining!

View dinner as a chance to reconnect, to recount the day's happenings, to share what's on everyone's minds, and to interact with each other in a way that you may not do any other time of the day. At your table, there may be joy and laughter or perhaps some sorrow and tears. In any case, you'll want to approach mealtime as an opportunity to solidify relationships, show affection, and lavish tenderness and love.

When I think back to our family meals when I was growing up, it isn't the food that I recall as much as the laughter, conversations, and storytelling that took place both during and after the meal. (Could it be that we were allowed to talk with food in our mouths?) The supper table was a place to linger, stay put for a bit, and continue our stimulating discussions. We also enjoyed the joking, teasing, and bantering back and forth about every subject imaginable.

When a teacher surveyed the young students in her classroom to find out how many had a regular sit-down meal with their families each night, she was appalled by the results. Not one child said they had dinner together every night and very few said they sat at the dinner table as a family for any of their meals. Most ate in front of the television or at a fast-food restaurant, and many ate alone. How sad it is that we are too busy to dine with our families at the end of the day. Or, is it that we do not recognize the value of family mealtime? Choose to dine rather than simply eat. It's possible on more nights than you might think. "Meals are small acts of great importance," Alexandra Stoddard prompts us, "moments set aside for conversation, reflection, and communion."

TREAT YOURSELF
LIKE COMPANY

*If I had my life to live over again…I would
eat more ice cream and fewer beans.*

BROTHER JEREMIAH

s I write this segment, I am sipping orange-spice tea
from my favorite china mug, a cherished birthday gift
from one of my sisters. Painted on its surface is a tranquil beach scene with a still lake in the background surrounded by
beautiful flower gardens behind white picket fences. In the fore-
ground is a cozy striped canvas lounge chair waiting for someone
(could it be me?) to curl up for a snooze. Robins are splashing in the
birdbath, and a pretty tray with afternoon tea is set out on a wicker
table. Yes—all of this on one mug! How restful I feel merely gazing at
it. If ever there was a picture that made me want to break from reality
and step inside for a brief respite, it's this one. I would cross over in
an instant if it were possible. But because it isn't, I am thrilled, at
least, to be able to enjoy this cherished mug filled with the aroma of
orange and spice, and use my imagination to retreat to that garden.
At one time, I would have placed this precious and treasured gift in
the china cabinet to be used only when a special friend stops in for
tea. Now I know better. I've learned to treat myself like company.

Why do we save our very best for others? If you have meaningful
possessions, whether it's fine china, crystal goblets, silver candle-
sticks, or ornamental napkin rings, get them out and take pleasure in
using them. Place your fine linens where you can view them and

decorate with the elaborate lace doilies handed down from your grandmother. Light your best candles—you can get more. Make a fire in the fireplace even if you're the only one home to appreciate it. Have your morning juice in a stemmed crystal goblet and your coffee in a fine china cup with saucer. Put fresh fruit in the cut-glass pedestal bowl that's been on display in the china cabinet. It takes the same amount of effort to serve yourself in your very best dishes as it does to use the chipped china and plastic bowls. You will feel so much better about life when you pamper yourself in these small ways. As an added benefit, there's no extra cost involved.

Spend a few minutes one afternoon going through some of your belongings—drawers, china cabinet, closets, hope chest—and see what's in there that is too good to use. Get out those things you've been saving "for later." Whether it's a satin peignoir set or silk pajamas, lace-trimmed guest towels, a cut-glass candy dish, or a designer silk scarf, start indulging yourself. What on earth are you saving them for? None of us knows how many days we have been given to live on this planet. Once you are in heaven, wouldn't it be sad for someone to find all those treasures, hidden within your home, never used or enjoyed?

As a mom, you are an expert at creating exquisite moments for others. You know how to take the ordinary and transform it into the extraordinary. Now it's your turn to experience the delight of being pampered, nurtured, and cherished. As the words in a well-known poem remind us, "Instead of waiting for someone to bring you flowers, plant your own garden." Everything you need to grow a beautiful garden is already there, waiting to be discovered.

LEAVE MARTYRDOM BEHIND

"If you trip over all those clothes on your bedroom floor and break both your legs, don't come running to me!"

hile I can't say for sure, I imagine my mother hollered the above disclaimer more than a few times while raising five daughters. I do know I said it to my own daughters when they were in their teens, and they will probably keep the tradition going with their own kids. A martyr mom couldn't stand that kind of mess in her kids' rooms. She'd be in there cleaning up day after day until the kids left home (and returned, and left home again). But it was John Rosemund who made the statement, "If you bend over backwards for your children, you will eventually lose your balance." Martyrs do have their place in our world, but if you want to stay poised, it's probably best not to be one in your home.

Whenever I read the verses on Hallmark cards that refer to the long-suffering, selfless, patient, and everlasting love of a mother, it's easy to see how we get moms and martyrs mixed up. When I came across one description of a martyr, it went like this: "a willing sacrificial victim suffering for a cause." Well, I checked out those words in my thesaurus and dictionary, and here's what I found:

> *Willing:* agreeable and compliant
>
> *Sacrificial:* surrendering, resigning, or succumbing
>
> *Victim:* wounded or injured party, a target of attack

Suffering: enduring or tolerating agony, misery, hardship, distress, or torment

Cause: a reason, goal, purpose, or intent

Now here's my question: What is your reason, intent, or purpose when you agree to resign yourself to being an injured party who endures distress and torment? Let's face it. Being a martyr is a choice, and not a very appealing or effective one. The truth is you are not doing your kids any favors (or anyone else for that matter, including their future spouses!) by being a compliant, wounded target tolerating agony!

Instead of continuing to live in the kingdom of martyrdom, start holding your children responsible. Ask for help when you need it. Let them know that being part of a warm, loving family also means helping out regularly with household chores. Teach them the necessary skills and you will see their self-esteem soar. You may even free up some time for yourself. As someone once wisely said, "If you want to see what your children can do, you must stop giving them things." On the other hand, if there are times when bedrooms and toy rooms get temporarily out of hand, and there's genuinely no time, or you're too exhausted to be the motivator, just close the door! Refuse to let it get to you. As my mom often reminded her five daughters, "This is not a hotel, and I'm not your maid!"

Teach the kids to brush their teeth, brush their hair, and brush the dog, but not with the same brush. The dog resents it.

PEGGY GOLDTRAP

AWARDS, REWARDS, & ACCOLADES

Give yourself a hug!

hen you need a hug, a boost, or some words of encouragement to keep you going (and there's no one available, or in the mood, to offer it to you), reward yourself! A friend of mine presents herself with an occasional "Mommy Medal of Honor" that she wears on a ribbon around her neck for a day when she's taken the kids to the library, finally organized a bedroom closet, or made a nice supper. She also owns a bejeweled plastic tiara so the kids can call her "Queen" for a day. Another friend buys herself trophies whenever she feels she deserves a little recognition—for extra hard work or a job well done. She has them inscribed, too, with the title of her choice—Thrifty Shopper of the Year, Five-Minute Clean-up Champion, Smith Family's Greatest Mom, or TCBW (The Country's Best Wife). Be creative and think of something you want to celebrate about yourself. Then make your way over to your local trophy shop. If you feel a little reluctant about paying tribute to yourself this way, no one has to know it's for you. Although, I'm sure if a woman is helping you at the trophy shop, she'll appreciate knowing. She may just need a boost today! So many moms are starving for a little recognition, acknowledgment, and appreciation for a job well done. Very few actually get it.

This is not about being vain, conceited, or proud. It is about having some fun, taking yourself lightly, and giving yourself permission to honor the contributions you make to your family, home, and community. It's for those days when you feel as though nothing you do is appreciated, or even noticed, and your job as a mom has turned into toil and drudgery. It's for the times you are worn out, weary and exhausted; when you feel you can't pick up one more pile of dirty socks from under the sofa, or change one more poopy diaper. It's for the days when you're longing to hear "thank you" or "well-done" or "you sure are appreciated around here," and you know it's not coming. While it may be understandable that you would be hesitant about celebrating yourself this way, it sure beats the alternative—waiting around for your husband and kids to notice the good job you've been doing, or complaining to anyone that has ears, including Rover or the gerbil, about how nothing you do is appreciated.

Jot down a list of some of the rewards you could use to treat yourself and keep it handy. When you have overcome procrastination, achieved some goal you've been putting off, or accomplished anything you feel deserves some recognition, check out your list. When you've finally cleaned off the piles on top of the refrigerator, enjoy a long soak in the tub. If you've managed to complete three loads of laundry including folding, have a cup of swiss chocolate almond coffee, light a candle, curl up, and read a magazine. If you cooked healthy, wholesome meals two nights this week, call an old friend for a gabfest, or if you helped out in your child's first-grade class, or baked heart-shaped cookies for the Valentine's Day party, get your hair done. If you romped on the floor with the kids instead of doing any of those things, pat yourself on the back and then go to the mall to buy a new nail polish, your favorite perfume, some lacy lingerie, a music CD, or a bouquet of fresh flowers!

In my former career, I was a national sales trainer with several large, direct sales companies. These days I am often hired as the keynote speaker at conferences for similar organizations. What I have noticed is these businesses attract women, many of whom are moms. Although there is the potential for incredible earnings, the reason many stay in these positions has more to do with the recognition they receive for their efforts. Awards and accolades are given out on every occasion. Aside from tangible prizes, sales representatives receive rounds of applause and standing ovations at every meeting, and managers are continuously on the lookout for opportunities to recognize accomplishments.

In your role as mom, rather than hoping you'll be called up on stage to be presented with a trip to Vegas, a diamond ring, or words of gratitude, honor yourself in small ways when you know it's deserved. Give yourself a rave review, a round of applause, a standing ovation, and a medal or two. Other people might think you're crazy, but who cares. You're the one with the trophy!

DRESS FOR COMFORT

*Amazing! You hang something in your
closet for a while and it shrinks two sizes!*

magine what it would be like to look in your closet and find only clothes that are comfortable, fit you perfectly, and make you feel good when you wear them. If you are like many women, little red indents all over your body when you get undressed at night are a good indication that you were probably not very comfortable during the day. Undergarments that are too tight and waistbands that dig in are bound to make a difference in your facial expressions, your attitude, your overall demeanor, and your performance. In my seminars on stress-free living, I occasionally ask audience members how many are wearing shoes that are too tight and pinch their feet. Invariably the hands of many women go up, and the men look at us as though we are crazy. Why would anyone wear shoes that hurt? Squeezing our body parts into uncomfortable clothes that tug, choke, pull, pinch, and hike up or down, makes us crabby and short-tempered. Beyond that, we are constantly being reminded of our figure imperfections. What would we be like if we dressed to feel good rather than to look thin or project the right image?

We could take a lesson from our children. They don't tolerate any of this. Although they can drive us to distraction being so persnickety, they know better than to go through an entire day feeling irritated. They base their clothing decisions on what *doesn't* pick, poke, scratch, or itch. If the seam in one sock isn't positioned exactly right, or the label on a T-shirt is irksome, off it comes.

As a writer, I find I do my most productive work in the early morning or very late at night, so I am often wearing my housecoat as I sit at the computer. But now I find myself wondering if I am doing my most productive work *because* I'm wearing my housecoat! I am certain that we perform at our very best when we are snug and relaxed.

Think about women's fashion images that are presented to us. Through magazines, catalogs, store ads, and commercials, we are bombarded with the latest trends, styles, and colors, plus fashion techniques that help us to look 10 pounds thinner. What we don't often hear is how to dress comfortably. "How do I look?" has always been the question rather than, "How do I feel?" Can you imagine what would change if you dressed to feel good and forgot about presenting the right image?

Dressing for comfort around the house does not mean looking like a slob, wearing only the shabby, tattered, and scuffed items from the back of the closet that have been retired from public appearances. Looking unkempt and bedraggled and wearing threadbare rags can be harder on our self-image than those clothes that tug, pinch, and pull. Get rid of those pieces or save them for painting the house or doing messy yard work. When you purchase new clothes, shop with the intent of adding comfort to your wardrobe.

You know what your comfort clothes are and what they look like. Yours might be the polka dot flannel pajamas you'd wear 24 hours a day, 7 days a week if you could get away with it. They're the cotton-knit sweaters, fleece-lined sweatshirts, downy bathrobes, loose-fitting jeans, and oversized shirts. They're the soft cotton undies that make you feel as though you're on vacation.

This week, go through your closet and take inventory. What pieces do you automatically reach for when you need to feel cozy, relaxed, and snug as a bug in a rug? On the days when you are especially tense, have PMS, are fighting a sore throat, or feel as if you are coming down with something, what would you wear? Think about how you would dress when you need some TLC. Make your list of what you need to fill in the gaps and jot it in a small notebook.

Include what you'd like to wear when relaxing in the evenings, running errands, going to the park with the kids, or hanging out with friends. Clip and add pictures from magazines and catalogs whenever you can. Create a collage of your new comfort wardrobe. Carry your notebook with you and refer to it as you shop.

When you clean out the old, you make room for the new. Getting rid of your uncomfortable clothes gives you the freedom to invite comfort into your life. When you do, it will show—on your face, in your eyes, in your posture, and in your radiant smile!

DO NOTHING

To do nothing is also a great healer.

HIPPOCRATES

s moms, we're convinced we have to keep on the move or else we'll lose momentum and won't be able to get our engines started up again. If we do consider taking a breather, we start to have scary visions of ourselves lollygagging around the house all day wearing tattered bathrobes and fuzzy slippers, with giant curlers in our hair, and eating gallons of rocky road ice cream right out of the container. We can almost accept slowing down for the purpose of doing something relaxing or comforting, but stopping to do nothing seems inexcusable. We simply cannot justify *doing nothing*.

A good friend reminded me, "If you don't stop when you need a rest, God may put you to bed." When we push ourselves to the brink of exhaustion, we are asking for disaster. We are aware that taking a break to do nothing periodically is what safeguards us against getting sick, making serious mistakes, and having accidents. But if your toddler has just spilled a bowl of oatmeal across a freshly washed kitchen floor, or you've got loads of bedding to wash because your son threw up three times during the night, it's difficult to grant yourself permission to do nothing. Certainly, there will be times when the situations and details of your life will not allow you to take a few moments to do nothing, but be on the lookout for those occasional moments when it is possible.

Believe it or not, there are some natural breaks in your day, when it would be convenient to do nothing. For example, between two tasks on your to-do list, when the baby goes down for a nap, right before the kids arrive home from school, after the dinner dishes have been cleared, or the last few moments at night before bed. Just for today, try it out. Actually schedule time for this. Take 5 minutes periodically to quiet your mind, sit down right where you are, and do absolutely nothing. Turn off the TV, radio, and answering machine—anything that might distract you. This doesn't mean you'll be turning your mind off. That's not necessary in order to make this a beneficial experience. Instead, allow your mind to focus on relaxing things, anything that would soothe you and bring peace to your body and soul. Gaze at a calming, restful wall hanging; stare out the window; look at pictures of family, friends, and pets; say a prayer of thanksgiving; and meditate on the good aspects of your life. Close your eyes and mull over fond memories of extraordinary occasions and the special people you've shared them with, or dream about plans you have for an exciting event coming up. Most importantly, don't allow yourself to think about anything even remotely stressful.

Be prepared for your mind or your body to balk. You'll feel sleepy or hungry. You'll think of a dozen things you think you should be doing or would rather be doing. Resist the temptation to give in and remind yourself it's only 5 minutes. Set the timer if you must. It will probably take some practice but the rewards are invaluable. Not only will you get your momentum back, you'll also be recharged, able to accomplish more in less time, and be a more enjoyable person to live with!

AH...COMFORT FOOD!

As I see it, a balanced diet is a cookie in each hand!

think I have found inner peace," someone reported to me not long ago. She explained, "I read an article that said the way to achieve peace is to finish things I have started. So today, I finished two bags of potato chips, a coconut cream pie, a case of soda, a bag of cookies, and a box of chocolates. I'm feeling better already."

Undeniably, food can provide the peace and serenity we long for, with relief for our aching hearts and disgruntled souls, albeit only temporarily. The flip side of it is that polishing off an entire bag of Oreos between the grocery store and home (making it necessary to stop off at a dumpster to dispose of the evidence!) also brings guilt, a big dose of self-hatred, and an onslaught of self-punishing exercises. When our inner critic floods our minds with condemnation about our irresponsibility, some of us have been known to throw the remainder of a dozen donuts out the car window as we go whizzing down the freeway, as a last ditch attempt at preventing ourselves from finishing them off. Then, we go home and force ourselves into neck-to-knee body shapers and clothes that are too tight—constant reminders that we have behaved badly and must be reprimanded. (If we don't feel bad enough, some of us go back after dark to retrieve the donuts.)

However, when eaten in moderation, we can use food for comfort without it becoming a harmful sedating influence. What comes to mind when you think comfort food? Peanut butter cookies warm from the oven? Macaroni and cheese casserole, chocolate milk, or butterscotch pudding? For you, it might be tomato soup and grilled cheese sandwiches, lemon meringue pie, or homemade maple fudge. I think of spaghetti and meatballs, chocolate brownies, or late night toast and jelly with a cup of hot cocoa topped with marshmallows. Usually comfort foods are the familiar ones you had as a child. Typically, they are full of fat, carbohydrates, and empty calories. But they are also the ones we reach for when we are feeling overstressed, overworked, overextended, overwhelmed, and underappreciated.

Imagine what it would be like to eat what you want without guilt. For starters, remind yourself that no food is bad. The words low-fat, salt-free, and high-fiber certainly make positive guidelines, but you may eliminate words like *fattening, high calorie,* and *prohibited* from your vocabulary. Imagine eating without diets and limitations, because you fuel your body regularly with balanced nutrition, so you're able to tolerate a little sugar and fat now and again. Think about why you are craving certain foods. Sometimes merely having an understanding of where this need comes from helps to curb the desire. There is obviously a very strong message to be heard when we eat half a pan of brownies fresh from the oven before the family gets home and then are forced to either finish them up and wash the pan (leaving a telltale phantom brownie scent in the air), or bake another pan and stash the leftover half to enjoy secretly later on (not that I've ever had to do it!). This latter idea makes us look especially good. With a whole pan of untouched brownies cooling on the counter, it appears as though we haven't even been tempted to sneak a taste. (Oh, come on. You've never done this?) The other alternative is to throw away the ones you didn't eat to get them out of your sight. Note: Wrapping them tightly in foil or Ziploc bags before you throw them out does not count. In fact, it's a good idea to douse them with coffee grounds, liquid dish soap, or some other inedible substance to assure there is no going back for nibbles when the cravings start up. Putting them in the freezer is not a solution either, because they don't take long to thaw. They taste good frozen anyway.

Or we tell ourselves, "If I don't eat this, I'm just going to keep picking away at it till it's gone, so I might as well eat it and get rid of it so I'm not tempted anymore." (Note: Only true comfort food lovers will get this reasoning!)

Whether comfort food for you is ice cream or cookies, over-indulging almost always ends up in self-hatred (and bulging cheeks—all four!), when what you really need is some healthy self-care. Nurturing ourselves in other ways can take the place of stuffing our faces. Try indulging in something you might consider frivolous—browsing through a home decorating magazine with your feet up, enjoying hummingbirds at a feeder outside your window or chick-adees splashing in the birdbath, working in your flower garden, watching an English mystery on TV, or just sitting and doing nothing. Craving comfort food is often related to feelings of not being cared for. When you choose to nurture yourself, you can begin to alleviate this need.

When you do choose to indulge in some comfort food, don't settle for less than what you really want and go for the best. If it's chocolate, make it Belgian; if it's pasta, have the richest sauce and lots of cheese. Order French toast stuffed with cherry cream cheese for breakfast. You can have a healthy meal later. Choose one weekend to forget about fat grams and calories. Eat anything and everything you crave. You need an occasional break from careful, controlled eating just as much as you need a break from working. A friend of mine lets herself off the hook with a T-shirt that says, "Hand over the Twinkies and no one will get hurt!"

TAKE A WALK ON
THE WILD SIDE

*It's never too late to be what you
might have been.*

Rather than take a risk, most of us would choose the safe route, the path of least resistance, if given the choice. Whenever possible, we opt for what is familiar and controllable. Sometimes it's out of fear—of the unknown, of failure, of making fools of ourselves. Other times it's simply that we've fallen into a rut born of the routines of day-to-day motherhood. So much of what we do daily is repetitive and habitual, as though we are operating on automatic pilot. Because we are in a place of comfort, we feel more secure saying no to others or even to ourselves when new opportunities do arise. We choose the mundane. We go for the plain, gold hoop earrings, for example, rather than the flashy, ornate clip-on ones we passed up at the flea market, fearing we would look overdone. Yet it is exactly those glitzy, flamboyant ones that we admire when we see another woman wearing them.

Every day you are given opportunities to embrace the new. It could be trading in the ponytail for a smart, sleek, classical cut that compliments your features. It might be choosing to wear a denim skirt with red cowboy boots instead of the usual blue jeans and sneakers to the next family reunion.

Make the choice to take a risk rather than play it safe. We could take a lesson from our toddlers. Children tend to seek out "uncomfortable" situations and explore new opportunities naturally. They find adventure in every seemingly impossible situation. They instinctively know that they must at least attempt the impossible in order to grow. When visiting our baby granddaughter, Alexandra, after she had been walking for only a short time, she decided to go from one side of the room to the other by squeezing herself into the small space between the chair I was sitting on and the wall. How much easier it would have been for her to simply go around the front of the chair. But there was no challenge in that, so instead, she pushed and shoved, huffing and puffing until she finally made it through to the other side. When she did, she flashed me the biggest grin that said, "I did it!" Her face beamed with a smug look of satisfaction and she looked so proud of her accomplishment. It was a victory she would have missed had she taken the easy route.

Take a chance. Do something out of character. Think of what people least expect of you and do it! Indulge in a secret desire you've suppressed or do something crazy you've never had the courage to do. Sign up to take a class—line dancing, woodworking, or choir. Order a cappuccino at lunch if you've never had one. If you've always listened to classical music, buy some jazz, gospel, or country CDs. Attend the ballet or live theatre if you never have. Switch from wearing traditional, classic styles and basic colors to those that are more flamboyant. If fiction novels have been your choice, try a good autobiography.

When you go someplace you've never gone before, you venture out of your comfort zone; when you try something new, you expose yourself to possible failure. You are an artist, your life is a canvas, and you are a work-in-progress. As Agnes de Mille reminds us, "Living is a form of not being sure, not knowing what is next or how…the artist never entirely knows. We guess. We may be wrong, but we take leap after leap in the dark."

CONFIDING
FRIENDSHIPS

Every true friend is a glimpse of God.

LUCY LARCOM

riendships with other women encourage us to grow. As moms, we especially need to forge bonds with other mothers who share similar experiences. Friends not only help us to see the best in ourselves, but they validate our emotions, reassuring us we are not crazy after all. They also remind us we are not alone in our struggles. The unfortunate reality is that with our active and demanding schedules, spending time with girlfriends is sometimes the first thing to go.

You can make an effort to stay close by calling or E-mailing friends regularly. A 5-minute chat can work wonders. Make a lunch or play date once a week with someone who understands the ups and downs of motherhood. Arrange a day when you can go out for breakfast and run errands together while the kids are at school. Consider organizing a *girlfriends-only* weekend. See if you can leave the kids at home with your husband: let him know you'll reciprocate for him one weekend. As an added bonus, he gains a new appreciation of what you do all day!

Occasionally seek out new friends. If the school your children attend, or the neighborhood or townhouse association where you live puts on special events, attend one. It's a chance to get to know people you already have something in common with—and they live nearby! Take some time to look up old friends, too. Times change, people grow apart, and we become involved in our own lives. It's a natural course of events. There are probably people who played a special role in your life who are no longer part of it. Whether it's your best friend from high school, a former coworker, or your hairstylist who used to listen to all your woes, they'll be as happy as you that you made the effort to contact them. If you had a great rapport with someone at one time, you probably still do. Call and reminisce.

If you can't track down a friend, there are Internet websites where, for a fee, you can search for long-lost pals. It's also fun to reconnect with childhood group leaders and former teachers who made a positive impact on your life. It will give you a chance to let them know how much you appreciate the role they played in your life. Don't be afraid to make the first move. Whether it's asking a potential friend to coffee or arranging time to see old friends, take the initiative. People are always saying, "Let's get together," but they seldom do. Waiting for someone else to do it almost guarantees no response.

When a friend has made an extraordinary impression or influenced your life in a special way, write down the qualities you love and appreciate the most. Acknowledge your appreciation by surprising your friend with a handwritten note expressing your feelings or by presenting her with a small token of your affection such as a bouquet of her favorite flowers, a scented candle, a new book or CD, or something to add to whatever she collects. It was Mary Kay who said, "I think there is something wonderful about everyone and whenever I get the chance to tell someone this, I do."

HEAVENLY IMPERFECTION

God saw all that He had made,
and it was very good.

GENESIS 1:31

Think about this verse—after completing the universe, God looked over all He had made and declared it *very good*...not perfect! Once a good friend of mine who had tapped the joy of imperfection taught me a valuable lesson: A life spent seeking perfection leaves little time for enjoying the big picture.

At the time, my life was out of balance in every way imaginable, but I had the cleanest house in town. Many of you reading this will understand precisely what I am talking about. It was as though I knew this was one area of my life I could completely control. With everything else being in a condition I found to be unmanageable, I needed to totally control some part of my life in order to stay sane. The problem was that I drove everyone else crazy: "You can't sit there—I just fluffed those cushions"; "If you pick up that magazine, I expect you to put it back on the pile with all the edges lined up"; "Don't walk on the carpet—it's just been vacuumed and I don't want to see footprints." Clothes were hung on the line in order of color or size. Books were lined up on the bookshelves in much the same manner, and I insisted they be replaced that way. Cleanliness and order had become an obsession. A woman came up to me during one of my seminars after I shared this story and confessed to being even more neurotic than I was. Apparently, on top of all of the above, she made sure there was a slice of lemon floating in the dog's dish at all times! Now I had to agree—that *is* being a bit fanatical!

Recently, I told my husband that it's too bad he didn't know me in those days, because people used to say you could eat off my floors. Today, you really could—it's like a smorgasbord. There are dozens of things down there to choose from! (Actually, the truth is I believe in creating job opportunities. The cleaning lady is coming next week and she might as well have something to do when she gets here!) These days I am so relaxed I tell the grandkids they can write their names in the dust, but not to put the date—no one needs to know how long it's been there!

The pursuit of unrealistic perfection signals that there's something going on inside of us: low self-worth, a poor self-image, feelings of not being good enough. These may have been derived from messages we received as children or images we continue to get through magazine ads, newspaper articles, television shows, commercials, and movies. The next time you flip through a magazine and see a picture of a home decorated to the hilt, a woman with a figure to die for, or a flawless meal supposedly prepared in less than 10 minutes, remind yourself it's all been created by professionals who spent hours attaining just the right look (or it's been airbrushed into perfection!). Let yourself off the hook and declare yourself *very good* even though you're not perfect. "Excellence I can reach for," wrote Michael J. Fox. "Perfection is God's business."

PART 4

AWAKEN YOUR SENSES

DELIGHT
THE SENSES

*Beauty satisfies the senses completely and at the
same time uplifts the soul.*

FRANZ GRILLPARZER

hether it's watching a beautiful sunset, enjoying a
scented candle, snuggling in your coziest pajamas,
eating something yummy, or listening to beautiful
music, we can benefit by recognizing, developing, and making the
most of the wonderful gift of our five senses. To make your 5-minute
retreats come alive, delight in what you can see, smell, touch, taste,
and hear.

See the grandeur of your surroundings. Observe the flame of a
flickering candle, and notice the patterns it casts on a wall. Browse
through a coffee-table book featuring a place you've always wanted
to visit. Stroll through a local garden center, and notice the wide
variety of colorful hues. Sit in the lobby of a beautiful old hotel and
study the architecture, or go out into your own backyard late at
night and watch the stars.

Smell the familiar scents of fresh bread, muffins in the oven, a
turkey roasting, clean sheets, new books, and old leather. Our sense
of smell, more than any other sense, has the ability to connect us
with memories, calm our minds, and revive our tired spirits. What
scents evoke the most memories for you? Is it coffee brewing or
bacon cooking in the morning, a certain perfume, freshly mown
grass, wood smoke on a late fall afternoon, or lemon oil on wood

furniture? For me it's baby powder, newly turned earth, and pop-corn. In a journal, list your favorite aromas and make it a point to enjoy them. Put some fragrant potpourri in a bowl; simmer cin-namon, cloves, and dried lemon peel on the stove; or light a vanilla-scented candle. Use a perfumed body lotion in the morning and lightly spritz scented linen spray on your sheets. Hang lavender sachets in your closet and from your car's rearview mirror for a calming effect.

Touch the clean sheets on your bed, a silk scarf on your neck, fur-lined gloves, or a fine leather sofa. Stroke your dog or cat. Have a massage, facial, or pedicure. Soak your feet in a warm tub and then rub them with a rich peppermint lotion. Run barefoot through the lawn sprinkler in summertime. Touch is our most important sense, and we would die without it. We need to be touched and to touch others. It is a powerful communicator that can actually improve our well-being. At bedtime, tickle your children's arms with a feather or write love messages on their backs with your finger and have them guess the words. In your family, tousle hair and give lots of kisses and hugs. Hold hands around the table when you give thanks.

Taste a hot drink—orange-spice herbal tea, hot chocolate with cinnamon, or Swiss almond coffee topped with whipped cream. Treat yourself to some freshly squeezed orange juice. Bite into a juicy, ripe peach or try kiwi fruit or a pomegranate if you never have. Introduce new flavors to your children. It's too easy to get in a rut with our taste buds and opt for the same old menu items. Eat mind-fully and really taste your food.

Hear the sounds of your family. Maybe sometimes you wish you didn't have to! But as Dr. J.A. Holmes put it, "A baby enters your home and makes so much noise for 20 years you can hardly stand it—then departs, leaving the house so silent you think you'll go mad." For now, really listen to the baby cooing in her crib, your tod-dler's giggle, and the kids talking in the next room. How does it make you feel when you hear your husband's car pulling into the driveway, someone yelling, "I'm home!," or your son's key in the door late in the evening just before curfew? Family noises can be comforting, giving us a sense of stability and reassuring us that all is as it should be. What are some of the sounds that bring back familiar childhood memories for you? For me it's a train whistle in the night, a screen door slamming, a teakettle whistling, and the creaking of a rocking chair. I love to hear the wind outside when I am snug indoors, or the rain beating a rhythm on the roof. Familiar songs at Christmastime, hymns in church, and the old favorites my parents would sing around the piano as Dad belted out the tune also bring fond memories.

Using all your senses is a healthy way to nurture and comfort yourself. Take advantage of this amazing gift. Tap into the pleasures of what you can see, smell, touch, taste, and hear. Imagine the emptiness we would experience if we were suddenly deprived of our senses....

SEE LIFE THROUGH
A CHILD'S EYES

Minor things can become moments
of great revelation when encountered
for the first time.

MARGOT FINTEYN

What joy it is to watch your child experience the "firsts" of life—the first kitten, the first snowflake, the first ant crawling along the sidewalk. How thrilling to see through a child's eyes the brightly clad clown in a parade, or a dazzling fireworks display, or animals at the zoo. Children approach each experience with a sense of awe and wonder. They view life as a breathless voyage of discovery. They notice what we don't. To a child, a scurrying chipmunk is a miracle; so is a maple leaf floating to the ground, a Popsicle melting, and wet sand at the beach. A child marvels at an airplane in the sky, the shape of popped corn, a honeybee on clover, or the feel of a cooked carrot being squeezed through clenched fingers.

What causes you to marvel? "You know you're old," says Merry Browne, "when you've lost all your marvels." To gain a fresh perspective, treat yourself to a roll of black-and-white film and take pictures of things around your house or yard that you would normally never think of photographing. Ask the kids for help on this one. Get their opinion as to what would make a great picture and see how children have a way of reinventing your world for you. As you study your photographs, you may find you are encountering minor things for the first time! Be ready for some moments of great revelation.

Spend time observing your children. They are great teachers and too often we miss their lessons because we fail to attend class. Children know how to genuinely have fun. They can spend hours playing make-believe and are intimately in touch with their senses. As I watch our grandson, A.J., climb on a chair and jump off with arms flapping wildly before he lands with a thud on the carpet, I realize he isn't hoping to fly, or wishing he could fly. In his boyish innocence and boundless imagination, he *is* flying! How often do we let life pass us by while we are *hoping* to achieve something, *wishing* for something to happen in our life, *wanting* desperately to experience the stress-free existence. Until it does, we believe we cannot be happy. Instead, in our mind's eye, we need to live the life we want. In our imaginations, we can see ourselves as the people we want to be—wild and fun loving on some days, tranquil and at peace with the world on others. We may land with a thud the first few times, but we can pick ourselves up and try again.

Try to recapture some of the impressions and sensations you experienced as a child. Ask yourself these questions: What was your most-loved book, fairy tale, or movie? What television shows were popular, and which ones did you like most? What food would you eat every day if given the chance? What was your favorite thing to do on your birthday or on a Saturday? What was your best vacation or the most memorable meal you ever ate? And the most important question: Which of these would bring you pleasure today? It might be to go barefoot, skip rope, turn a somersault, catch snowflakes on your tongue, swing from a branch, or put on a pair of rubber boots and splash in a rain puddle. Reactivate those wonderful feelings of childlike enjoyment. Reconnect with that part of you that is still a child yearning for fun, adventure, and love.

See life through a child's eyes and let yourself be overwhelmed by the most innocent pleasures life has to offer. Become a sponge and soak in even the simplest of life's details that you normally overlook. Soon you'll be observing the beauty in objects all around that you typically take for granted. When you start to see life anew every morning as a child does, you might say to yourself as Bernard Berenson did, "Each day as I look, I wonder where my eyes were yesterday."

REFLECT ON THE SPLENDOR AROUND YOU

The sky is the daily bread of the eye.

RALPH WALDO EMERSON

*H*ave you ever received a postcard from a place so beautiful you longed to put yourself in the picture? Perhaps you stopped for a moment to imagine what living every day in such a location would be like. When that happens to me, I become convinced that doing mundane chores like packing lunches, folding laundry, changing diapers, scrubbing toilets, and vacuuming must somehow be a lot less monotonous in Hawaii, Rome, or Tahiti.

The truth is, there is beauty all around us no matter where we live. Even people living in the most magnificent surroundings can become oblivious to the richness of their environment when the tedious details of daily living take over. One day, I happened to catch a glimpse of a television commercial for a vacation destination that looked like it would be a magnificent place to visit. I watched to the end so I could jot down the name of this beautiful place. You can imagine my surprise as I discovered it was my own hometown, and I hadn't recognized it!

When my husband and I first moved to our country property, we were convinced that being consciously aware of the quiet beauty of the woodlands surrounding our house was something that would never wear off. We believed we could not help but notice it each and every day. However, we found there were many days when we were so caught up with the daily grind of getting the kids to music lessons, picking them up from sports practice, helping with science fair projects, and shopping for new shoes, that we didn't notice the splendor all around us.

Being aware of the wonder when it is close by does require a certain mindfulness and deliberateness. It is something we must decide to do. This awareness may come more easily to you if you already live in a place you consider to be beautiful, or if you have had the opportunity to move to a particular place because of its beauty. If you live somewhere that requires you to look a little deeper to see the beauty, you may need to redefine majesty and splendor. With a little conscious effort, you will soon find yourself in awe of a winding, tree-lined rural road while driving the kids to baseball practice, freshly made snow angels in winter, or the sparkle of sunlight glistening on a backyard wading pool.

It's not necessary to travel to exotic lands or even to leave your home to experience real beauty. Sometimes it's just a matter of perception. Stand by a window or step outside onto the porch for a few minutes. Observe the miracle of a flower pushing its way through a crack in the sidewalk. Notice the lines, colors, and textures of nature all around. Allow the brilliance of sunlit autumn leaves to take your breath away, or watch a flag gently sway in the breeze. And remember, there may be a visitor out there sending someone a picture postcard of your town!

ALLOW NATURE
TO NURTURE

*Surely there is something in the unruffled calm of
nature that overawes our little anxieties and doubts:
The sight of the deep-blue sky, and the clustering
stars above, seem to impart a quiet to the mind.*

JONATHAN EDWARDS

In our living room is the jasmine plant I purchased as a gift
for my husband one Christmas. He was introduced to this
aromatic plant at a friend's home and was attracted to its
beautiful, sweet-smelling fragrance. At the moment, its tantalizing
aroma fills the room. I often catch a glimpse of Cliff bending over the
blossoms, breathing in the delicate perfume.

Even if you are not able to spend the day outside, you can bring
nature indoors. It can be as easy as adorning your home with a
variety of user-friendly houseplants, a beautiful spring bouquet from
the market, or a single exquisite flower. Pick up a variety of small
vases and put a few blossoms in each one. Choose artwork for your
home that reflects the things in nature that pacify you—streams,
rivers, and waterfalls; forests, flowers, and woodlands; sunsets and
storms; birds and butterflies. You can also purchase a cassette with
nature sounds set to a background of classical music. Lie down near
a window and allow the warm sunshine to saturate your body.
Nature slows us to a more relaxed pace. It tempers our worries and
cares. Allow the calm to soothe away your stress and nurture your
thirsty soul today.

When I am completely overwhelmed with life, I am drawn to
nature. I find myself standing in my kitchen, looking out the

window at the cardinals, blue jays, and finches that come to visit one of our many feeders. There's also the birdbath that attracts as many small animals as it does birds. Squirrels and chipmunks scurry up for an occasional drink, and birds flutter and splash in their morning bathing rituals. Raccoons often visit to snack on the residue underneath the feeders, and a deer with her fawn will venture out of the woods to nab an apple or two from the tree next to the house.

"In all things of nature, there is something of the marvelous," said Aristotle. When you are feeling sluggish or off-kilter, find some natural delights to lighten your mood. Keep field glasses and a bird book by the window and also in your car. Learn to identify the chirps and warbles of a few different species of birds in your area.

Even if you live in the city and have little contact with nature, there are ways to connect with the grandeur of the outdoors. When you arrange to have lunch with a friend or dinner with your husband, plan a picnic in the park or your own backyard instead of going to a restaurant. One evening, spread a blanket and lie on the grass under the stars or watch cloud formations in the daytime. Notice how patterns of light filter through tree branches and dance on the lawn. Feel the breeze against your skin. Go outside at night and watch fireflies or observe a crescent moon on a brilliant starry night.

As a child, the camp I attended each summer provided cabins, but there was one special night for campers to sleep outdoors. We snuggled inside warm sleeping bags as we watched the moon, studied the stars, and sang camp songs. It was an awe-inspiring and memorable experience. My children have fond memories of the summer nights they slept on lounge chairs on the balcony of our old apartment. Why not sleep outdoors one summer night?

When you pine for the tranquility of nature, follow your instincts. Plan a nature getaway—walk on the beach, go to a park, or find a nearby patch of woods. As Lord Byron declared, "There is pleasure in the pathless woods." Visit a greenhouse, garden center, or florist shop. Breathe in the humid air and the aroma of moist earth, linger over the flowers, and delight in the splashes of color you'll see there.

Nature is an equalizer, helping us to maintain our balance. When you escape all the paraphernalia and synthetic trappings of modern living, you leave behind the whole realm of striving and struggling.

Anne Frank wrote in her diary in February 1944, "The best remedy for those who are afraid, lonely, or unhappy is to go outside, somewhere where they can be quiet, alone with the heavens, nature and God. Because only then does one feel that all is as it should be." Nature is God's silent wakeup call that all of life can be enjoyed.

IT'S AUTUMN—TURN
OVER A NEW LEAF

What is Autumn? A second spring,
where the leaves imitate the flowers.

ALBERT CAMUS

utumn may represent the end of summer, but I've long thought of this time of year as the ideal season for making a fresh start. There's a break in the weather, the kids are going back to school, and there is the promise that some sort of order may be restored to your household. It's a natural point in time for new beginnings. Unlike making New Year's resolutions in January when we are worn out, broke, overweight, and just want to hibernate, in the fall we are fresh from the reprieve of summer. It's a good time to determine what changes you'd like to see happen in your life. Would you like more time to be alone with your husband, with your children, or with friends? Are you longing for a more organized, clutter-free environment or a simpler lifestyle? Perhaps you'd like to take up a new hobby, learn how to play a musical instrument, or start walking more regularly. Get yourself a "fresh start" journal and put your hopes, dreams, desires, and goals in writing.

Since the stores are now filled with a wide assortment of school supplies, treat yourself to some of your own—a crisp new notebook, lined scribbling pads, a three-ring binder filled with clean paper, yellow pencils, pink erasers, and the best pen you can afford. Add some scissors, tape, a ruler, and a brand-new box of Crayola crayons just for fun. Now go ahead and make your "new season" resolutions!

If you've been blessed to live in a four-season climate where the leaves change, take a drive through the countryside to see fall's flamboyant array of brilliant red, yellow, and orange leaves. Even in Florida and southern California, you can find leaves that change. Make it a fall ritual in your family to travel somewhere, if only a few miles, to see the changing leaves. Notice the gardens, too, and how they seem to be at rest now, as though they are saying, "We've done our job, now leave the rest to nature."

Set aside time for adventures with kids. Take a walk in the dazzling autumn sunshine or in the evening when the aroma of burning wood fills the crisp air. Walk briskly, inhale the fall air, and kick the leaves. Collect some leaves to take home. Run through a tall cornfield, go for a hayride, fly a kite, or let the wind push you down the street! Stop at a roadside stand and let the children pick out some apples—Golden Delicious, McIntosh, or Granny Smith. Then go home and make apple muffins, applesauce, or apple crisp to be dished up warm with vanilla ice cream. Buy some fresh apple cider and serve it hot with cinnamon sticks. Kids love to use them as stir sticks or straws. Make taffy apple pie by melting caramels to pour over the top of a homemade pie or one you've picked up at your local market.

For dinner, set a seasonal table and adorn it with small pots of mums, gourds, dried flowers, and leaves you have collected. Temporarily preserve the leaves by placing them between two sheets of waxed paper. Cover the top sheet with a cotton tea towel, and press them with an iron on medium setting until waxed sheets melt together. When our children were small, we always made a giant autumn tree by drawing or painting the trunk and branches on a large piece of poster board, and then taped our newly waxed leaves all over it. Of course, it was hard to tell what type of tree it was since the leaves had been collected from a variety of trees!

Scoop out pie pumpkins—the midget variety—and put votive candles in them for your dinner table, or use them as natural vases to make mini-arrangements of fall flowers. Fill them with a florist foam first, add your arrangement, place on a tray, and surround with waxed leaves. The kids can make one to take to their teacher.

Continue your decorating outdoors. Use hollowed-out pumpkins filled with pots of mums or votive candles to line your front steps, walkway, or porch. This is a good time to plant a few tulips, daffodils, and crocuses for next spring.

Get out your favorite cozy sweater or shop for a new one. Gather everyone and have a leaf party—a time of raking crisp leaves into piles with the sole purpose of jumping into them. Do you remember doing that as a child? The scent of the leaves is something that lingers for a lifetime. Celebrate autumn all over again.

ENJOY WINTER'S WONDERLAND

In winter we lead a more inward life. Our hearts
are warm and cheery, like cottages under drifts,
whose windows and doors are half concealed,
but from whose chimneys the smoke cheerfully ascends.

HENRY DAVID THOREAU

If you live in a climate where you must brave the frigid, frosty climate of wintertime, you might think of this as a season to hunker down and hibernate until it passes, especially if you're not one to enjoy outdoor sports. Although it can be comforting to stay indoors, snuggled by the fireplace with your hot chocolate and a good movie, consider some outdoor activities. To brighten the days, seek out farms that offer horse-drawn sleigh rides through the woods. Or, bundle up the kids, find a frozen stream, and have fun ice-skating. Pick a spot to have a winter picnic, and build a blazing bonfire, roast hot dogs, and toast marshmallows. Play in the snow—make a fort, build a snowman, go tobogganing or sledding, or have a snowball fight. When you're done, go inside, wrap up in quilts, curl up by the fire with mugs of hot cider, and relive the day. If you really can't get outdoors for your picnic, spread a blanket in the living room, and cook hot dogs or toast marshmallows in the fireplace.

On a snow day, when school is canceled, stay home with the kids if you can. Lounge around in your pajamas all day. Make hot chocolate with real cocoa topped with miniature marshmallows or whipped cream, and shaved chocolate curls. Play board games. Remind yourself that this is a gift—an unexpected vacation!

When it gets close to Christmas, take pleasure in the delicious holiday food. Enjoy eggnog, a piece of rich, buttery shortbread, or a slice of Christmas pudding with warm caramel sauce. Bake some Christmas cookies. Have the kids cut out their favorite shapes and top them with sprinkles. (You can purchase ready-made dough!) Set aside an evening with your family or a few close friends for a Christmas film fest and watch *It's a Wonderful Life* or *Miracle on 34th Street*. Go caroling in your neighborhood. Friends of ours do this every year, stopping by the homes of seniors, shut-ins, or people who have endured a recent tragedy. With the help of local churches, they assemble a list and then plan a route. They make it open to anyone who wants to brave the cold, provide some special joy for their neighbors, and have fun at the same time! Recently, this group arranged to have a horse-drawn carriage take them to each destination, which made it even more enchanting when people came to their doors. After caroling, invite everyone back to your home to warm up. With your house aglow from the glimmer of Christmas tree lights, the flicker of candles, and a blazing fire, linger over cups of cider and talk about what the season means to you.

This is a good time to make some decisions about gift giving. Maybe you can cut back on shopping and arrange to do something special together as a family instead. We have been doing this for the past few years, and it has tremendously reduced the pressure we used to feel during the holiday season. Each family pays their own way, and we go to a lodge that offers a wide selection of winter activities including tobogganing, ice skating on an outdoor rink, hiking trails, and dog sledding. There's also an indoor pool and game room with a ping-pong table. We spend our evenings sitting by the fireplace, playing board games, and munching on popcorn. We even cook our own turkey dinner complete with all the trimmings. As our grandson A.J. commented, "Gifts wear out, but memories last forever!" Why not pick an event you could attend or an interesting place you could go for a weekend getaway or a family trip?

You may want to exchange simple gifts—a game for the whole family to enjoy, something that you've made yourself, theater or sporting event tickets, a gift certificate from a favorite restaurant or for pampering services people may not usually indulge in. Just a few small stocking-stuffers or fun gifts you've picked up at the dollar store are also economical. Consider creating coupons for someone special. Give a friend the gift of time away while you watch her children, or present your husband with a coupon for a free neck and shoulder rub. Choose some Christmas events to attend—school concerts, the much-loved Nutcracker Suite ballet, or church musicals and dramas that depict the true reason we celebrate Christmas: the birth of Jesus. Amid the tinsel, cards, carols, chocolates, candy canes, and toys, set aside some quiet time to reflect on God's ultimate gift to you. Share your blessings by donating to a shelter or by making a dream come true for an underprivileged child.

Winter truly can be a wonderland! Besides, as the British poet Percy Bysshe Shelley noted, "If winter comes, can spring be far behind?"

SPRING INTO SPRING

It might be spring,
but who's getting a break?

fter a long, lingering winter, especially if we have been cooped up indoors with a rambunctious family, we are more than ready for a spring break. Although you may not be able to actually get away to some dream vacation spot, there are ways to rouse yourself from the doldrums and breathe life into your stifled soul after surviving the frosty winter months. While the natural world wakens from a long winter's slumber, revitalize your spirit at the same time by bringing some of spring's brilliant beauty indoors.

When I was a child, at the first whisper of spring, my mother would make a celebration of airing out our stuffy home after the long winter. She'd put on some lively music, throw open all the windows, and let the drapes blow in the spring breezes. The ritual of "spring cleaning" began with the airing of carpets and blankets, washing curtains, and polishing streaked windowpanes. What I remember most is the way she would brighten the rooms of our modest home with cheery bouquets of daffodils, tulips, and lilacs set in colorful vases, and large pottery jugs filled with bright yellow forsythia branches. If you don't grow these spring beauties in your own garden, bring home a few bunches from the market or florist, or pick them up from a street vendor. They are a wonderful way to bring spring indoors.

Enjoy the exhilarating new birth all around you. Walk around your neighborhood and look for fresh growth—blossoms, buds, bulbs, and grass shoots. Notice how branches, which just days ago were bare, are now blooming with delicate leaves. Take a country walk through a meadow and gather bunches of pussy willows, or pick some up at the florist. Make a garland for your front door by tying them together with florist wire. Add a flamboyant, brightly colored bow with long streamers to the bundle that will flutter in the spring breeze.

On a rainy day, curl up with a cozy afghan and listen to the raindrops on the roof. Or, put on your rubber boots, grab an umbrella, and go outside to splash in mud puddles. Later, when the rain has stopped, turn over the earth in your garden and delight in the smell of the damp soil. The scent of the earth reawakening will stir up your sleepy spirit. When the weather is clear, sit on a breezy, sun-drenched porch and have a few friends over for an afternoon tea party.

Celebrate Mother's Day by letting your children know how special they are to you. Relive stories of their birth that they love to hear over and over again. Write a love letter to your own mom if she is still alive, telling her all the things you want her to know. In fact, write it even if she is not.

After a long winter's slumber, spring ushers in feelings of hope and the promise of a fresh start. Hope is a crucial element in human nature. It is something we cannot live without. We must have hope that things can improve. I heard about an interesting experiment in which two groups of participants were put into separate rooms and instructed to place their hands in buckets of ice water. They were told not to wear watches but that someone would be back to get them when the experiment was over. While the length of the experiment was to be 3 minutes, only one group was told this. The other group didn't know how long they would have to endure the cold. When the experiment was over, the group with no time frame could not even last 3 minutes whereas the other group said they could have gone on even longer if necessary. The reason? They were the ones with hope!

Cross the threshold of spring with hope, with positive expectations, and anticipation of better things to come. With God, all things are possible. Doesn't He remind us of that truth as the whole world awakens once again every spring? What an appropriate time for Easter—a holy day when we rejoice in the resurrection of Jesus, our Savior. Buy an Easter lily for your home and each time you see it, remind yourself of the new birth that has been promised to you. Celebrate life…celebrate spring!

SUMPTUOUS, SPECTACULAR SUMMER

Summer afternoon—to me those have always been the two most beautiful words in the English language.

HENRY JAMES

No season evokes nostalgia more than summertime. Do you remember the long, carefree afternoons of your childhood summers? Lying on the cool grass, you gazed up into the clouds and saw a prancing pony, a roaring lion, a clown with a big nose, or a train with giant puffs of smoke drifting off into the sky. We think we don't have time for such childish pastimes these days, but once summer arrives, try to pare down the activities on your to-do list. Stretch out in a hammock on a midsummer afternoon to gaze into the sky. Do it whether you're alone or with your children. Relax and get comfortable as you allow your eyes to explore the heavens. Delight in spotting a kitten scampering across the sky, a galloping horse with flowing mane, or any other wonder that may be hidden in the clouds.

One clear evening, camp out with your family in the backyard. Lie on a blanket or snuggle in sleeping bags to enjoy the sparkling beauty and boundless magnitude of the night sky. Nothing spells out eternity and puts my life back into proper perspective quite like a clear, starry night. See how many of the constellations you can find. (The Big and Little Dipper are usually the easiest to spot!) When I consider the timeless stars, galaxies, light years, and unfathomable distances, I am convinced that God has everything in His hands and He is in control. We can find comfort—a sense of order and well-being—in the heavens.

Later on, pitch your tents and spend the night together. Make a campfire for roasting hot dogs, and introduce your kids to s'mores for dessert. Do you remember how to make them? Place pieces of a chocolate bar on a graham cracker; toast a marshmallow and place it on top of the chocolate; then put another graham cracker on top. Eat up and enjoy!

Summertime activities and opportunities are endless. If you live near the woods, look for dancing stars—fireflies—illuminating the sky. At twilight, catch these lightning bugs in a jar with holes punched in the lid, just remember to let them go later. Listen to nature's chorus of chirping crickets and croaking frogs.

Keep beach towels, water toys and sunscreen handy, get to the nearest beach and have a sandcastle building party. Search for shells on the shore while you are there. Back home, use sidewalk chalk and draw a funny picture or a game of hopscotch. Teach the kids how to make daisy chains or a paper fan to keep cool. Make your own Popsicles from fruit juice and eat them outdoors. Let them drip all over your hands and off your chin, then hose down before going inside. Sit on the back porch and eat giant slices of chilled watermelon. Afterward, have a seed-spitting contest!

One evening, put the kids in their pajamas and go to a drive-in movie. Treat everyone to pizza and popcorn (you can take your own!). On a Sunday afternoon, find a small tourist town where you can take a horse-drawn carriage ride. Rent, or borrow, a bike if you don't have your own, and take a tour through a quiet neighborhood. Seek out a strawberry festival in your area and indulge in a giant serving of strawberry shortcake topped with mounds of real whipped cream. Take the kids to a "pick your own" fruit farm so they can see where fruit really comes from. Go to a traveling circus or visit the local zoo. On a sultry, sweltering, steaming summer day, sit in a rocking chair on the veranda sipping iced tea or lemonade poured from a frosty pitcher. Watch a summer thunderstorm from a screened-in porch and play piano nocturnes in the background. You may want to doze off for a short catnap.

Lazy, hazy summer days—a time for old-fashioned potluck picnics, fireworks, and parades, and a time to slow down and reflect. As a mom, you probably don't get a three-month vacation, but you can indulge in simple pleasures that can help you recapture the joy of good old summertime!

TAKE A FANTASY VACATION

*Many have no happier moments than those
they pass in solitude, abandoned to their own
imagination…which shifts the scene of pleasure
with endless variety, bids all the forms of beauty
sparkle before them, and gluts them with
every change of visionary luxury.*

SAMUEL JOHNSON

When you've got the kids-drive-me-nuts, the washing machine's-broken, I-banged-my-knee, just-ate-a-whole-bag-of-cookies, and might-as-well-curl-up-and-watch-television blues, that's a good time to take an imaginary trip. If you feel you need an escape more than ever, but you know that a real vacation is probably out of the question, at least anytime in the near future, you can benefit from an *armchair retreat*. Amazing as it sounds, the benefits you gain from taking a fantasy trip can be nearly as powerful as if you had gone on a real journey. Here's why I'm so sure about that: If you have ever awakened from a nightmare in a sweat, with your body trembling and your heart pounding, you were reacting physically to what was happening solely in your mind. Your body responded as if what just occurred in your dream was the real thing, even though the experience was imaginary. A fantasy vacation works much the same way, but in reverse. Unlike the nightmare encounter, your body, mind, and soul will experience positive outcomes and beneficial results—feeling calm, relaxed, energized, and refreshed.

Sit in your favorite comfy chair, settle in, and close your eyes. For this trip, put monetary restrictions and physical limitations aside. Why go economy? Imagine that you have been given unlimited resources to plan your dream vacation. Go first-class all the way. Tell yourself you can take as long as you wish—a weekend, two weeks, or a month—and you can visit anywhere you choose. Consider an exotic place you'd like to be right now—a white, sandy beach on a sunny deserted island, a cottage by the lake, a cabin in the mountains, a rain forest, a sailboat on the Caribbean. Then, imagine that you are there. Examine each detail. Envision yourself walking around your vacation spot. Fill in the particulars, appealing to all five senses. What are the smells you'll enjoy—the flowers and trees, and coffee brewing? Where would you eat dinner? What foods are on the menu? What is the weather like? Can you hear waves lapping against the shore and feel the warm sunshine? The more details you can fill in, the more you will benefit from your imaginary trip.

"The soul without imagination," said Henry Ward Beecher, "is what an observatory would be without a telescope." To limber up your imagination, visit the library for books about where you would go on your dream vacation. Log on to websites that allow you to virtually visit places you may not have a chance to see otherwise—the Louvre in Paris or a waterhole in Africa. Collect travel brochures, maps, and guidebooks about places that interest you. Gather together a sheet of poster board, a pair of scissors, and a glue stick and make a dream vacation collage. Borrow or rent travel videos of some of your fantasy spots. After you've watched them, you'll feel as though you've actually visited those places!

Sometimes we get so caught up in the demands of daily living that the only fantasy we ever have is that the laundry will get caught up or we'll have one good night's sleep, or the next light will turn green before we get to it. We tread wearily through our days, putting one foot in front of the other, asking ourselves what difference it would make to dream anyway. God, the great Creator, has made you with incredible creativity. So, allow your imagination to take you away from the daily grind, at least temporarily. When you do, you'll come back invigorated.

YOUR BATHROOM—A RESTORATIVE SANCTUARY

There is no sanctuary of virtue like home.

EDWARD EVERETT

f your children are small, you may cherish your moments in the bathroom because they may be the only time you have to yourself. As a place of restoration and revitalization, you'll want to make this room as appealing and inviting as possible, and just as beautiful as any other part of your house.

Keep a pretty basket filled with your favorite inspirational booklets and decorating, gardening, or cooking magazines to browse through during a relaxing late-night or early morning soak in the tub. Displaying small bowls of fragrant potpourri, guest soaps in their original wrappers, and other little treasures you've collected will lift your spirit and help you return to the household with a more gracious attitude and a cheerful disposition. Candles, photographs, a touch of lace, and a swag of greenery around a window or mirror make the room warm and cozy, and can be enjoyed by everyone in the family. Aside from lighting bright enough for applying makeup and shaving, position a low-watt lamp in the corner to add a warm glow and a pleasant decorator touch.

The bathroom should be a restful and romantic spot because it is a place of both solitude and sharing. A tub big enough for two makes a welcome setting for a chat to catch up with your husband at the end of the day. One couple we know has made a point of doing this as a nightly ritual for the 35 years they have been married, including all the years they were raising their three youngsters along with several foster children. A young mother shared with me recently that when her four-year-old son and twin toddlers set the household on spin cycle, she takes them all into the bathroom, lights some candles, runs a foamy bubble bath, and plops them in the tub together. Then, she sits and relaxes while basking in the candlelight, browses through a magazine, or reads from a favorite novel while the little ones play.

At the end of the day, what could be more soothing and relaxing than sinking into a tub of warm water for a long, luxurious soak? Soften the water with scented bath salts or add some fragrant bubbles, and you'll hardly notice that you're surrounded by bright yellow rubber duckies and drinking your tea from a colorful Disney character sippy cup!

UNPLUG THE WORLD

*I find television very educating. Every time
somebody turns on the set, I go into
the other room and read a book.*

GROUCHO MARX

ometimes we simply need a break from modern technology,
whether it's the television, stereo, alarm clock, car radio,
phone, fax, pager, or computer. Mr. Marx had a good plan.
Simply leave the room and do something constructive. Most of us
don't. I think we get so accustomed to these conveniences that are so
much a part of our homes, jobs, and lives that we become anes-
thetized to their influence.

One morning while walking by the lake, I passed by a mother
strolling with her little boy. As the mom talked nonstop on her cell
phone, the little fellow chattered incessantly to her, pointing out sail-
boats in the bay, wild geese and ducks along the shore, fluffy white
clouds in the sky, and the big red-and-white lighthouse at the end of
the pier. When he stopped for a drink at a water fountain, mom
clumsily lifted him up with her one free hand without missing a beat
in her conversation. As they continued on their way down the path,
I felt a strange sadness come over me. While the little one appeared
oblivious to the fact his mom wasn't listening at all, I couldn't help
but think about all this mother was missing. This moment in time
was one she would never get back.

More than 200 years ago, the poet William Wordsworth made the
statement, "The world is too much with us." When the world is too

much with you, priorities become distorted and values become skewed. Perhaps a weekend or even one day without the trappings of modern technology would do us good. I believe it could help immensely in reestablishing priorities, ideals, and standards that are important to us. Such a time would be a wonderful opportunity for recovering balance, joy, and spiritual strength.

As moms, we not only have little people demanding our attention from the time we step out of bed in the morning until we collapse back in it at night, but we also have timers on stoves, buzzers on washing machines and dryers, beepers on answering machines, and the ringing of telephones all relentlessly reminding us that something needs to be looked after. Just for a day, turn off the ringer on the phone. Let voicemail take the calls. Pay no attention to time. Don't set your alarm clock or wear a watch. Forget checking your E-mail. In fact, don't even turn on the computer. Leave the television, radio, and VCR turned off, too. You may even want to go so far as to turn off the lights and enjoy some candlelight.

Our world has a sense of urgency about it. While we may not be able to change that, we can control whether or not we allow the clamor to affect our private worlds. Plan your escape for a day and take time to ponder, muse, contemplate, and reflect on what real living is all about.

PART 5

SIMPLIFY, SIMPLIFY, SIMPLIFY

Simplify, Simplify, Simplify

Life is a great bundle of little things.

OLIVER WENDELL HOLMES

This current generation of moms has taken multitasking to the extreme. We do it mainly because it comes naturally to us, but also because we're good at it. We are flexible and adaptable by nature, so we keep taking on more and more. This can come in handy with our full schedules, but we need to stop multitasking to the point of ridiculousness. It's one thing to accomplish a few tasks at once by using a cordless phone to chat with a friend while tidying up, folding clothes, or unloading the dishwasher. On the other hand, if we have to wash our pantyhose while we take a shower (especially if we're still wearing them!), or clean the grout in the tiles with an old toothbrush while we wait for our hair conditioner to work, we may have gone too far. One woman I know does deep knee bends while using the curling iron, and another lifts weights with her free hand while brushing her teeth.

Although this could be considered effective time management, it can't beat what I saw the other night while watching an infomercial. It was for an electric-twirling hair-styling brush. The woman demonstrating it made the comment, "I know our moms taught us to brush with 100 strokes every day for healthy, shinier hair, but with our busy lives, who has the time for that?" I am not kidding! She then went on to show how this brush was the answer to our problems. I think we are in big trouble if we can't even manage the time to brush our own hair properly without the use of an electronic gadget!

In all fairness, if you are thinking, "That's me! I just ordered that brush," I have to admit to a time when I had newborn babies, it would sometimes be five o'clock in the afternoon before I managed to use a toothbrush, hairbrush, makeup brush, lint brush, or any other type of brush. So I know what it's like and that's why I've come up with some suggestions.

Here are some rational and realistic ways to simplify your days. Start at bedtime the night before. Tidy up and leave things in order for the next day. An organized kitchen, bathroom, or desk make for a smooth start in the morning. Invest in a haircut that suits your face shape, hair texture, and lifestyle. You'll know it's a good one if it doesn't take more than a quick brushing in the morning and you can style it in 20 minutes or less the day you shampoo. Try to complete one load of laundry every evening. That way, you never have laundry day with its endless washing, drying, and folding, not to mention putting it all away. Do as much shopping and banking over the phone as you can. Order from catalogs whenever possible. I even get my best-fitting pantyhose through mail order. Stand in line less by avoiding high-traffic times: the days before and after a major holiday, suppertime at the grocery store, weekends at the shopping mall, Friday afternoon at the bank, and Saturday night at the movie theater. Run your last errand by 11 A.M., when parking is easier and traffic is less dense. Seek out services that streamline your time—a dry cleaner that picks up and delivers, an online grocer, or a complimentary personal shopper that some department stores offer. Create a gift shelf somewhere in your home to avoid last-minute dashes to the store for birthday gifts. When my daughters were small, I bought two of everything, and also picked up gifts as I spotted them, knowing there'd be a party to attend sometime!

When you do simplify your life, you'll be freeing up time to savor more of the innocent pleasures of life like snuggling with a child in your lap, lingering over a magnificent meal, or watching a glorious sunset.

OVERCOMING BUSYNESS

*Our days are identical suitcases—all the same
size, but some people can pack more
into them than others.*

AUTHOR UNKNOWN

re you too busy, or do you have a *full life*? There is a big difference! When you say you are "too busy," it implies that something or someone outside yourself is influencing how you spend your time. On the other hand, proclaiming to have a full life suggests that you are in control of where your time goes. Although it may not seem like it, you do get to determine how full your schedule will be. Busyness is always a choice. The key is in knowing how you want to spend your time, what you really want to accomplish in a day and in a lifetime—what can be put on hold, what can be delegated to someone else, and what doesn't need to be done at all.

There's nothing wrong with living a full, productive life and even taking on new challenges. We can experience stress from positive events, too—a wedding, a new baby, a vacation. As one stress researcher Hans Selye said, "Stress is the spice of life." But sometimes things can go beyond what's tolerable. If you're like most moms, you are on the move from the moment your tootsies touch the floor at dawn until you flop into an unmade bed in the wee hours of the night. Between getting the kids off to school, trying to get a few things done around the house (you know, the stuff that normally takes 25 hours a day!), taking your turn as a parent volunteer, and then picking up dry cleaning, dropping books off at the library, and hunting down some material for a research project you're working on, you continually feel as though you're playing catch up.

Very few moms I know lead simple lives. Most are juggling multiple roles with home, work, family, friends, and volunteer activities. We tend to cram way too much into way too little time. When we do meet up with our friends and ask how they're doing, the common response isn't, "Fine, thanks," but "Busy, too busy."

While being too busy is draining, having a full schedule can also be challenging, but at least that is manageable. Days that are filled with a balance of activity, rest, and play are days filled with joy and meaning. This kind of busyness is healthy. There's also temporary busyness, the kind that comes in spurts and doesn't last forever—a major project with a deadline, a trip to the emergency room, a crisis in your family, and the pressures that go along with certain life stages: parenting preschoolers, launching a business, changing careers, or going back to school. My good friend tells me one of her favorite Bible verses says, "It came to pass." In other words, it didn't come to stay! This is the type of busyness we just have to muddle through, like caring for a sick child who's "throwing up" at both ends. We know that if we can somehow get through the night, things will eventually calm down again.

Then there's continual, unending busyness when we don't have the comfort of knowing when things will return to normal. Instead, it becomes the norm. This is the type of busyness that causes burnout. When you discover that your life is controlling you rather than you controlling it, something has to give. Too much doing, going, helping, and giving takes its toll on us—mentally, physically, emotionally, and spiritually. We neglect our own needs, run out of inner resources, lack the energy to invest in family and friends, and then wallow in guilt.

The main reason this happens is we put things that are important—our health, our souls, our relationships—on the back burner, and devote our time and energy to what is immediate and urgent—intrusive phone calls, last minute requests, other people's priorities. We find ourselves reacting and merely surviving rather than focusing on our true values. Think about what you value. Write it down and post it where you can see it. Once you know what you value, what you want to do and be in life, it becomes easier to say no to the urgent. This leaves you free to pursue the important.

Enough Is Enough

Health enough to make work a pleasure; wealth
enough to support your needs.

JOHANN WOLFGANG GOETHE

ow many times have you said the words "if only"? If only I had a bigger house, one more bathroom, more closet space, or a bigger kitchen. If only there were more hours in a day. If only I had a newer car, more exotic vacations, and could go out for dinner more often. If only I could sing and play the piano, had whiter, brighter teeth, and a deeper tan. If only my husband could be more like hers—any woman could be happy with a man like that! If only...if only...then I'd be satisfied. We are convinced we are missing out on something the rest of the world is experiencing, and we want what they have.

Once, when I was the keynote speaker at a huge entrepreneurial convention, I strolled through the halls during the coffee break and overheard a conversation between two women (actually, I was eavesdropping!). The first one stated that she was starting her own business in spite of the fact that she had eight children still living at home. The other responded, "Oh, if only we had eight children." When the first woman looked a bit shocked and asked her why, she replied it was because she has 12 kids! (Well, maybe in her case, she had a right to say "if only"!)

There's an ancient proverb that points out three things we must know to survive in this world: What is too much for us, what is too little for us, and what is just right for us. When we buy into the idea we don't have enough of what we need—whether it's time, money, help around the house, storage space, furniture and appliances, clothes and accessories, appreciation and respect, or love and affection—we go around constantly feeling deprived. It's as though life is passing us by before we get our turn to enjoy the good things we so desperately think we must have in order to be happy. But are these truly needs or merely wants? Someone once speculated the only reason many families don't own an elephant is that they have never been offered an elephant for a dollar down and easy weekly payments.

The next time you want to purchase an item you suspect is a want rather than a need, and it's more than 20 dollars, wait for three days. Talk it over with someone—your spouse, your kids, or a good friend. In three days, if you still feel it's a wise purchase, then go ahead and get it. But only by paying with cash or a check. You certainly don't want to go into debt for something that is a want rather than a need. Wants can also be placed on a list for gift suggestions or when you choose to budget extra money for them.

Recently I was having a conversation with a friend about the difference between our wants and needs. We concluded, while there's a big difference between necessities and requirements, sometimes the boundary does get blurred. Take 5 minutes and ask yourself what you really need at this moment. What would bring you true joy, contentment, and peace? It may be to slow down, to hug your child, to stroke a purring kitten on your lap, or watch birds flitting to and from the feeder outside your window. Maybe it's to relax over a delicious home-cooked supper in the glow of candles, read a captivating novel by a cozy fire, go out for breakfast with the family, work in your garden, or sit on a porch swing sipping tea with an old friend. More than likely, what you need is to feed your soul—with peace and joy, contentment and gratitude, and love for what you already have.

JUST SAY NO

Honey, I shrank my to-do list!

oms usually say yes. So it's only natural that our to-do lists keep growing until they are out of control. When we do have a little "leftover" time, we believe we can squeeze in more than is realistically possible. Have you ever been late because you got up early? In the past, I was almost always behind schedule and the main reason was because when I had a bit of extra time, I attempted to squish far too many activities into that slot. Most of us are poor estimators of time and how long a particular task will take. It's no wonder we're always rushed. Combine that with the inability to get the word *no* past our lips, and it's easy to see why we fall into the trap of filling our to-do lists with more than we could ever achieve and remain sane.

So how do we shrink those lists? Sometimes the one we need to say no to is ourselves. My new motto goes like this: "Never put off until tomorrow what you can avoid altogether." It takes a lot of awareness and practice before we get the hang of this. A while ago, several of our friends and their children were in the habit of getting together at each other's homes for a late-night snack on Sunday evenings after church. While it started out plain and simple, our snacks grew to become full-course meals complete with candles, linen, and a choice of three desserts. Eventually, it became too much for us. Our group consisted mainly of young moms and many had part- or full-time jobs. Although we appreciated and needed the fellowship, we couldn't keep up with the preparations or the expense. Gradually our evening get-togethers dwindled, and we missed seeing each other.

One day, I suggested that because it was the fellowship we really wanted, we could try again, and this time use the KISS formula: Keep it sweet and simple. Our plan was to serve nothing but tea and toast. Cliff and I hosted the first evening and it was a huge success. We actually placed the toaster right on the bare table, had one loaf each of brown and white bread, plus jars of jam and jelly for people to help themselves. Cliff asked guests which bread they wanted, popped it in the toaster, and passed it down the table when it was ready. We had such a carefree evening that night and everyone decided this was a good idea. My girlfriend hosted the next one and she served the same, but added bagels. The next hostess served all of that plus English muffins and homemade jams. The next one included fresh-baked banana muffins, raisin bread, and flavored coffees…and so on. Eventually, we were right back where we started! Why do we do this to ourselves?

We complicate things by saying yes to every outside request. We take on too much, and after it's too late, we realize we've bitten off more than we can chew. Then we complain about how everyone takes advantage of our generosity and willingness to help out. In reality, we have no one to blame but ourselves. We can make things easier on ourselves by cutting back, by making a conscious effort to condense, decrease, minimize, and shrink the items on our lists every time we get the chance.

This may mean being more assertive. You might have to practice what to say when you are asked to volunteer on one more committee. Try something like, "That sounds really interesting. Let me check my calendar and I'll get back to you." You can also say, "Thanks for asking, but it's not going to work for me at this time!" or "Normally I'd be glad to help out, but my schedule is already full." Before committing to extra projects, consider all your other obligations and responsibilities, and then decide if it is the best use of your time. There are going to be times when it is the right thing, and then you can say yes from a full heart, not merely from a sense of duty.

Perhaps we need to say no more often to our children, too. I wonder if we have a hard time doing that because of all the guilt we carry as a result of having such full schedules and not always being available. When we pare down our to-do lists, we will have more free time and will be able to say no without feeling guilty.

Here's something you'll probably never hear your grown children say: "Mom, I am so grateful you sacrificed your own happiness and personal satisfaction so that I could have everything I wanted. I'm glad you were miserable and that you never said no to me so that I could have my every need met. Thank you for not living your life to the fullest and being an example to me of what sacrificial living is all about. Now I plan to follow in your footsteps and give up any fun, pleasure, and personal fulfillment in my life when I have a family." You have the awesome opportunity to be a positive role model. Give yourself and your children the extraordinary gift of time. Do it by learning how to say no!

TAKE ONE
STEP BACK

I try to take one day at a time, but sometimes
several days attack me at once.

Most of us are running full throttle, climbing up the ladder of motherhood at top speed. We might be irritable, frustrated, bitter, resentful, burned out, and depressed, and we're not sure what's at the top, but we sure are in a rush to get there. We're always dashing and darting somewhere, and then hurrying and scurrying to get back again. What's behind all this rushing?

There are a number of sources. First of all, being busy is seen as a virtue in our culture. We wear it as a badge of honor. We admire others who can manage frenzied schedules between car-pooling and music lessons, do colossal loads of wash with a baby in one arm and a phone tucked under their chin, and we wish we could be like them. The ability to get more done in less time is one of our most sought-after values. We have fallen into the trap of "haste," and we call it convenience. While our washers, dryers, and microwave ovens have freed up our time, and we wouldn't want to be without them, we have been subtly programmed to believe that their purpose is to enable us to do more, faster than ever. Before you know it, we start to run our lives the way we drive our cars to the parent-teacher meeting we almost forgot about—too fast!

Modern technology has made it harder for us to slow down, too. Answering machines, cell phones, pagers, fax machines, and E-mail make us accessible to the world at all times. It's becoming increasingly harder to come up with a feasible excuse as to why people can't have what they need from you within the next few minutes.

Blaming technology and our society for our never ending scurrying doesn't solve the problem. In fact, the real problem is the impossible standards we have set for ourselves. We are often running on empty and out of breath because of our unrealistic expectations. We take on too much because we think saying no is a sign of weakness. We're wrongly motivated by thinking the more we accomplish, the better we'll feel about ourselves. We are human *beings*, not human *doings*.

When we feel like we're the only ones who can make something happen, we need to ask ourselves if we're doing it because we want to feel needed. Children can make their own beds and their own lunches, but sometimes doing it for them is validating for us. Besides, it's one more thing we can check off on our long list. Too often, we believe it is our responsibility to make everyone happy. Then when they aren't, it must be our fault. While you may be responsible *to* others, you are not responsible *for* them. Others get to choose their own happiness.

When we feel "too busy," our real need isn't to find ways to cram more into our already full lives, but to concentrate on what matters most. Not to live more efficiently, but more *effectively*. While we know it is important to be organized, efficient, and clutter-free, our goal should be to spend most of our time on what we value most.

How do you determine your true values? Take some time to think about it. In a journal, list the various roles you play—wife, mom, sister, daughter, friend, group leader, Sunday school teacher. Consider the hats you wear at home, at work, in the community, and in your church. Describe the very best "you" in each situation. What are the qualities you have to offer? List them and take note of any common themes. Single out those activities you feel you are the best at, the ones where you fully utilize your unique gifts and talents. You may be good at doing a lot of things, but when you have the opportunity to use your unique strengths, you are at your best. The sooner you figure out what they are, the quicker you can eliminate the activities you don't want to continue pursuing. The things you enjoy will become a lot easier to recognize. Maybe it's time to take a step down the ladder.

The best way to control your hectic pace is to realize you do have choices. If your days are too full, it's because you've filled them. Do yourself a favor and take one step back. It's your choice!

MAKE A "NOT-TO-DO" LIST

*Better is a handful with quietness,
than both the hands full with travail
and vexation of spirit.*

ECCLESIASTES 4:6 KJV

ost of us have lists—on the refrigerator, in our purses, on our desks, and on our calendars. But have you ever thought of making a "not-to-do" list? Ask yourself what you need to do less of to be more easygoing and relaxed, and write down your thoughts. Here's a hint: What you need less of is whatever causes you *vexation*—annoyance, aggravation, exasperation, irritation—of spirit. The opposite of vexation is what a not-to-do list can bring to you—feelings of satisfaction, fulfillment, pleasure, and contentment. Would it help to have less hurrying, scurrying, chaos, clutter, and confusion? Do you need less volunteer work, overcommitment, or doing for others? Maybe for you, it's less noise and commotion, junk mail, or junk food. Or, perhaps you'd like to reduce schedules, appointments, meetings, and messages. Consider which activities and things you could possibly release that would mean you'd have more peace and harmony in your world.

Devising a "not-to-do" list may mean turning people down. It might involve lowering your standards and expectations. Or, it could be a matter of being more patient, tolerant, and lenient—with others and yourself. I learned this the hard way.

One summer, I invited a family we know to join us for a backyard barbecue. To keep it simple, I planned to grill hot dogs, open a bag of chips, and serve ice cream cones for dessert. Since I was going to the effort anyway, I invited some other friends. Soon the group grew to several adults and children. Now, aside from hot dogs, we also cooked steaks, along with potato chips we had salads, and desserts became homemade pies. Suddenly, the patio furniture didn't look that good so I purchased some new pieces. The spare bathroom needed a facelift so fresh paint and wallpaper were ordered. I was out of control! Talk about *vexation of spirit*. Not only was I exhausted and broke, but by the time guests arrived, I felt as though I never wanted to entertain again.

Later that summer, I relaxed at a park while my grandchildren romped and splashed in the wading pool. Next to me on the park bench sat a young mom watching her little boy on the swings. Looking at her watch, she called, "Shane, time to go!" Shane pleaded, "Just 5 more minutes, Mama?" She nodded in agreement and Shane ran to use the slide. When time was up, his mother stood up and called again, "Let's get going, Shane!" Once more, the boy begged, "Just 5 minutes more, Mom. Please?" "Okay," his mom said as she smiled and sat down again.

I couldn't help but comment on what a tolerant mother she was. As a grandma, I now have that kind of patience, but as a busy young mom, I'm not sure I would have been as accommodating. Then she explained, "Before Shane was born, a car hit our little girl Emily while she was waiting for the school bus. The woman driver had a heart attack, her car went out of control, and they both died instantly. I always felt I was too busy to spend a lot of time with Emily, and now I'd give anything to have just 5 more minutes with her. I'm determined not to let that happen with Shane."

Maybe it's time to make your "not-to-do" list. Ask yourself if this were your child's last day on earth, what could be canceled or left undone so that you'd have more time to spend with him or her?

START A
COOKING CLUB

Alone we can do little;
together we can do much.

HELEN KELLER

hile catching up with a friend late one afternoon, we talked about what to cook for dinner that night. We both agreed with our full schedules, it was quite a challenge to prepare hearty, nutritious, home-cooked dinners on a regular basis. That was when she shared with me how excited she was about her newly formed cooking club that operates much like a Christmas-cookie exchange. It all began one Saturday when she decided to spend some time preparing several meals to put in the freezer for the week ahead. While working in the kitchen, she realized how simple it would be to make extra portions for her friends and their families. If they each did the same, they'd have a delectable variety of meals in the freezer for future use.

After explaining the concept to three friends, they were eager to get involved. Although they easily could have worked alone, they chose to plan their menus and make out their shopping lists together. After purchasing all the necessary ingredients, they get together in one friend's kitchen—a different one every two weeks, so each member's kitchen is being used once every two months—and spend time chopping, dicing, slicing, grating, laughing, and sharing.

Here's how it works: Each member makes three of her family's favorite main courses but multiplies the ingredients to make a total of four of each of the dishes. Once completed, they are placed in large freezer bags or aluminum pans covered with heavy-duty foil. The containers are marked with the contents and cooking instructions. Each cook keeps one of each of her own dishes and shares the other three. In total, every member goes home with 12 main courses. Combined with one take-out meal and one restaurant meal, there are enough dinners to last for two weeks. All that's necessary to turn each main course into a complete meal is a tossed salad, vegetables, and perhaps some bread, rice, pasta, or potatoes.

A cooking club is a simple and fun way to feed your family tasty home-cooked meals every night. Start with just a few people that have approximately the same number of family members, children about the same age, and similar tastes in food. (Otherwise, food might be wasted.) Use recipes that you've tried in advance, and you know will freeze well. Make a master list for yourself and check off what's been served, keeping track of what's left in the freezer. You may want to collect everyone's grocery receipts and divide the total by the number of families participating so the cost is the same for everyone.

A cooking club will reduce kitchen time, save money, and put more home-cooked meals on the table than ever before. But most of all, it's about the fun you'll have, the friendships you'll strengthen, and the knowledge you've made someone's day easier and your family meals more special.

CREATIVE TIME-SAVERS AND SHORTCUTS

Time given to thought is the greatest time-saver of all.

NORMAN COUSINS

f you want to enjoy more 5-minute retreats in your life, discover some innovative ways to free up the time you do have. One woman wrote to tell me, "My husband is always coming up with time-saving ideas for me. One morning when I was making breakfast, he commented on all the trips I made between the refrigerator, stove, table, and cabinets, often carrying a single item at a time. His *helpful suggestion* (he insists it wasn't criticism!) was to save time by carrying several things at once. Well, his suggestion did turn into a big time-saver. While it used to take me 10 minutes to make breakfast, he now does it in 7!" When you start getting creative, you'll discover all kinds of shortcuts to save yourself a little time.

Start your day on a smooth note by having everyone in the family lay out the clothing they'll be wearing the night before so there are no major decisions to be made in the morning. You can also have the children take turns helping you set the breakfast table at bedtime. Put out the bowls, glasses, silverware, cereal boxes, bread, toaster, and jam. Then, all that's left to do in the morning is take out the milk and orange juice, and the family can help themselves to a healthy breakfast.

When it comes to cooking supper, whenever possible, prepare double recipes of your meals—one to eat and one to freeze. You'll appreciate it later on. Keep the pantry stocked with items you use often—basics you'll need to make quick, last minute suppers, or for times when company drops in.

Reduce your kitchen-cleaning time by cutting down on the number of dishes you use for preparation. Mix salad dressing right in the serving bowl. Use just one bowl for baking by mixing the dry ingredients on wax paper and the wet ingredients in the bowl. Then add the dry to the wet, and blend them together. Develop the habit of filling the sink with hot, soapy water while you're cooking or baking for easy cleanup as you go. Line baking pans and casserole dishes with parchment paper or aluminum foil to save scrubbing later. To avoid sloppy spills, use extra-large bowls when baking, tossing salads, or mixing ingredients. Place the bowl in the sink if necessary. Use your 6-quart stockpot for mixing double batches of ingredients for potato salad, cookies, and casseroles, and also when using your hand mixer to prevent splatters.

Keep seldom-used information handy by hanging or taping charts on the inside of cupboard doors with stuff you need to know: equivalent measures, substitutions, roasting temperatures for various meats, and cooking times for particular dishes (in case you can't reach your mom!). Store your most frequently used utensils in a basket on the countertop or in an individual drawer. Put the ones you use least often in a separate drawer. That way, you won't be rummaging through a whole range of paraphernalia before you finally dig up the utensil you need. A shoe bag with plastic compartments hooked over the back of a kitchen door is a handy way to store large but seldom-used gadgets, spices, or cleaning supplies.

Use muffin pans for baking a variety of foods: stuffed peppers, potatoes, or apples. Soften a hard stick of butter quickly without melting it by grating it. Coat the grater with non-stick spray for easy cleanup. Use an ice cream scoop to remove seeds from a melon or winter squash and use scissors to chop parsley, fresh herbs, and dried fruit. Keep a new, clean powder puff in the flour canister for dusting flour on the rolling pin or pastry board.

With these shortcuts, cooking will be more fun, cleanup will be easier, and you may even find that spending time in your kitchen becomes one of the nicest 5-minute retreats of your day!

MAKE MEALTIME SIMPLE

*Countless people have eaten in this kitchen
and gone on to lead normal lives.*

In between car-pooling, attending your child's softball
championship, and completing the budget proposal for
next week's annual meeting, there's still chicken to be
roasted, salad to be tossed, and vegetables to be diced for supper.
There's no way you could make a gourmet-style meal every night of
the week, even if you did consider cooking dinner your favorite
retreat activity. However, there are ways to experience 5-minute
delights when you want to prepare simple, tasty meals.

For starters, choose make-ahead, no-fuss recipes. Get out your
slow cooker. You'll find that most recipes call for fewer ingredients
and a lot less work. Toss in a bit of this, a can of that, and leave the
cooker to work its magic. Get in the habit of using this kitchen gem.
Your family will appreciate coming home to a house filled with
savory aromas and a hearty meal on the table. There are hundreds of
ideas for slow-cooked meals ranging from down-home suppers to
fancy cuisine. Some recipes keep it simple, while others add gourmet
flair with a sprinkling of pungent herbs and a splash of cooking wine.

For those evenings when everyone gets home at the same time,
have some precooked casseroles in the freezer (yours or store-bought)
that can easily be popped in the oven and ready in 30 minutes or less.
Keep your pantry and refrigerator stocked with fast side dishes like

fresh vegetables and fruits, quick muffin and biscuit mixes, brown-and-serve dinner rolls, pasta, and rice. Take advantage of convenience items like ready-cut salad mixes, dressings, and pasta sauces, and mix them with your own seasonal fresh ingredients. It may cost a little more to buy foods that have been prepared for cooking in advance, but prewashed salad greens, skinned, boned chicken breasts, and peeled baby carrots all cut down on cooking time. That will help mealtime seem more like a retreat.

Keep the fuss to a minimum with these tips. Bake potatoes in the microwave oven, slice them in half and scoop the pulp into a bowl to be mashed with butter and milk. This means no peeling and cleanup is a breeze. Do the same with squash. Pierce it in several places with a sharp knife before cooking it in the microwave. Once cooked, it will be tender and easy to cut. With an ice cream scoop, remove the seeds and scoop out the squash into a serving dish. If you or your family pack lunches, keep bread fresh all week by dividing a loaf into sealable sandwich bags with two slices in each. Put these into a larger bag in the freezer. Each night take out one small bag per person and you never end up with stale sandwich bread!

Let yourself off the hook. Prepare simple, no-fuss, appetizing meals. Enjoy your retreat…bon appetit!

EFFORTLESS ENTERTAINING

*Being a successful hostess doesn't depend on
the external—the beautifully decorated home,
the priceless china, the gourmet food.
It depends on what's inside you.*

Ann Platz

ll too often when entertaining guests, I have found myself flying around looking after everyone else's needs and never really enjoying the party or tasting the food. Finally, when our guests were on their way home, I would settle down, make a fresh cup of coffee, and survey the leftovers. Before I knew it, I'd recklessly gobbled up the last lonely bacon-wrapped scallop, stuffed the remaining three cheese puffs into my ravenous mouth, scraped the few remaining tidbits of chocolate marble cheesecake onto a plate (or not!), and devoured it along with the wilted celery and dried-out cheddar cheese I almost overlooked. Ah, at last…I was almost able to experience what everyone else had been enjoying all evening, minus the best part—the fellowship.

I knew I had to change things so I could enjoy having guests in my home. I discovered that by making a few adjustments and alterations, entertaining could be fun and simple—even for the hostess.

Start by keeping a collection of recipes that are easy, tasty, and can be prepared ahead. My new motto: bake and freeze now to thaw and enjoy later. If time doesn't allow you to cook the entire meal, offer the main course and provide ice cream for dessert. Then, have friends bring their favorite toppings for making sundaes. They'll have fun, and you'll be impressed with how creative they can be! Or, go out to a restaurant for dinner and come back to your home for dessert. Try having just a dessert party. For dinner parties, we have found that by inviting three families, individuals, or couples, each contributing a portion of the meal, we entertain a lot more often. As the host family, we provide the main course, the second brings a salad, and the third supplies dessert. Encourage everyone to bring along their recipes so you can all share.

For larger crowds, plan a potluck dinner. There's no need to be shy about asking guests for a little help in putting together the meal. Our busy schedules have brought potlucks back in style. It's fellowship with food, and each cook gets to shine with his or her special dish. People don't seem to mind and often ask what they can bring along anyway. The old church social was on to something.

Progressive dinners are another option. You have appetizers at one home, soup and salad at another, the main course at the next, and finish up with dessert at the last home. You can follow the same pattern by visiting restaurants as well. Although it's more costly, there's literally no work for anyone.

Theme dinners are fun, too. Celebrate your family's cultural heritage or that of your guests. At our home, because my husband is of Polish descent, we play folk music, eat pierogi and cabbage rolls, and occasionally get up to polka! Whatever you choose, remember the KISS formula: keep it sweet and simple. After all, it's the fellowship we are craving!

CLUTTER-FREE AT LAST

Clean out the old to make room for the new.

hen I started to think about 5-minute retreats, I didn't want to consider the matter of clearing away the clutter. But the more I explored pampering and nurturing rituals, the more I realized it is nearly impossible to truly reap the benefits when you have to dig yourself out from under piles of stuff, or shuffle your way through mounds of junk. There seems to be an unspoken law that says we must release the old in order to create a vacuum to receive the new. When you want to get to a whole new level—whether it's more time for yourself, happier family times, better health, improved relationships, increased energy, or better finances—the way to get moving is to clean out the clutter in your life.

It's much easier to give yourself permission to take regular 5-minute retreats when you're not swamped with junk mail, tripping over toys, losing important papers, and tolerating mounds of clutter. Here's a test: If I were to call you right now and tell you I want to stop by, would you say "Sure, no problem," or "Okay, but don't look in this room or that closet," or "No way! Not until I tidy up." For some of us, tidying up means throwing everything into a box, shoving it in another room, and locking the door. Or, we make one giant sweep across the counter pushing everything into a drawer. There's a difference between being neat and being organized. Neat is when surfaces are clear. Organized means being clutter-free and able to put your hands on things when you need to find them.

There is also a difference between being a *neat freak* and being clutter-free. What I'm not talking about is living in a sterile environment, spotless and impeccable at all times, but rather creating an atmosphere that is comfortable, cozy, and looks lived-in minus the mess that causes confusion and makes us crazy. A neat freak is like the lady I heard about who met her hubby at the door every night and made him strip naked. This was not a matter of unbridled passion, but rather her way of getting his work clothes into the washing machine before he wore them into the house. Now, this poor fellow was an office worker—it's not as though he came home from a dirty factory! Another husband says that when he gets a glass from a cupboard and sets it on the counter, by the time he turns around to get some juice, his wife has put the glass away. He complains that if he gets up in the night to go to the bathroom, when he comes back, the bed is made. He also says she folds everything in the shape of swans—hand towels, napkins, paper towels, dish towels—and he's afraid to use any of it!

I'm not talking about that sort of fanaticism. What I'm talking about is clearing away what you don't need, don't use, and don't want. Start by making a quick game of 5-Minute Pick-Up. Rally the troops and get the kids involved. Set a timer, blow a whistle to begin, and see who can pick up and put away the most things in 5 minutes. Once everything is off the floor and the toys are put away, you will be able to see more clearly what has to be done.

When I do some serious decluttering, I use the four boxes and list method. The boxes are for collecting items and the list is to record cleaning jobs and repairs that need to be done. You don't want to get caught in the trap of doing these tasks during a decluttering session. Pick a room, closet, basement, attic, or any other area that has clutter, and go through it with your four boxes. Designate one box for throw-away, one for give-away, another for put-away, and the last one for storage. Make a decision about each item. Throw away any items that are broken or outdated, like old typewriters. Give away things that are still in good repair but you don't use them anymore. Maybe you have replaced them with newer versions or have duplicates (and you're just keeping the old ones for spare parts!). Store only those items that you know you will use in the future, but not on a daily basis. Be careful with this box—it may seem as though everything goes in this category. Items in the put-away box are things that are out of place and belong in another room. Put your own items away and give family members 24 hours to claim theirs. If they are not claimed, either hold them for ransom or let people know they will be donated to a worthy cause.

If all you have is 5 minutes, do what you can to clean out one drawer, cupboard, or closet.

Be prepared for the emotional pull of your clutter. We have many psychological attachments to our belongings and material possessions. Remind yourself you haven't missed your pink sweater you wore in high school in all these years, and the unfinished craft project isn't even something you're interested in anymore. For the give-away box, switch into a charitable mode, telling yourself that someone else will use it more than if you keep it stashed in a box in your basement.

After a day of sorting through the good, the bad, and the ugly, it will be time to set up some organizational systems to keep things tidy and enjoy order in your home. "Out of clutter find simplicity," said Albert Einstein. And simplicity comes naturally when you have order in your home.

ORDER IN THE HOUSE

*If it weren't for the last minute,
nothing would get done!*

as every morning become a scramble for your child's schoolbooks, notepads, unfinished homework, hats, scarves, and mittens? While it's no fun to begin every day like that, there is some good news: Disorganization is usually caused by habits and habits can be changed. Once you get organized by implementing some simple routines and systems, you and your family will benefit by having more free time and less stress. The end result—you have more opportunities for personal 5-minute retreats!

I have to admit that I am not, by nature, an organized person. I am a free spirit with an artist's heart and a creative mind. This has always been my excuse, and I'm sticking to it. However, the truth is that I detest disorganization. That's what prompted me to come up with a series of systems for getting organized and staying that way— at home and at work. I have had the opportunity to present these unique strategies and techniques at workshops across the nation. Although being organized still does not come naturally to me, I now have the tools and the knowledge I need to gain control. I know what to do when I see things becoming unmanageable again.

The credit must go to my home economics teacher, Mrs. Gallop, and a phrase she drilled into our class: "A place for everything, and everything in its place." She was right. I have finally discovered that when you put things where they belong, you don't waste time searching for your keys, the measuring cups, scissors, or envelopes and stamps, because you and everyone in the family know where they're kept. The key is for everything to have a place. That's usually where we fall short. We don't put things where they go because they simply don't have a home.

Once you have cleared away the clutter, now is a good time to set up some storage and retrieval systems. A workable system not only means you have a place to store items, but it also allows you to locate them quickly anytime you need to. If that is not the case in your home, here are a few suggestions.

First of all, let's deal with paper management. For those papers and documents you do want to keep, set up a simple file system. There should be no loose pieces of paper floating around your house. Place every paper you want to keep in a file folder. If a category doesn't exist, start a new one. Then, place all permanent papers in your file cabinet or drawer alphabetically. Separate different categories by using file folders of different colors. For example, children's school and health records in green, financial documents in blue, household utilities and expenses in yellow, and so on.

Consider having a different colored file folder for each family member. Using a stacking tray, assign one slot to each member, and insert his or her file. When there are messages, mail, memos from school, report cards, or anything that must be signed and returned, that's where it goes. People are responsible for checking their own files when they come home at night and again in the morning before leaving the house. There shouldn't be a problem with papers building up in those files because what you are using them for are transient items, not permanent papers. Continue on with the color-coding system with bins by the back door to keep mittens, keys, cell phones, and school bags organized. Have medium-sized, plastic laundry baskets for each member of the family in his or her color.

For permanent papers, try some of these ideas. Place manuals for small appliances, cordless phones, fax machines, and so forth with their coordinating warranties, sales receipts, and credit-card slips in plastic pockets that fit in a large 3-ring binder. Create a master locator sheet at the beginning of the binder, listing what is in each pocket so you can retrieve it at a glance. Set up another binder for your children to store all their artwork once it comes down from the refrigerator. This way they can have a beautiful book with just their drawings and paintings. Assemble several binders for yourself—for recipes that you clip from magazines, or for home decorating or gardening ideas. It's a great way to clear out all those magazines you've been collecting.

For items that need to go into storage, use plastic boxes and place numbers on the outside. On recipe cards, put the corresponding number and itemize the contents of that box. Put all the cards in a recipe file box. When you need to find something, simply glance over your numbered cards. In children's rooms, use small, see-through plastic boxes (rather than a toy chest), to store toys. Attach pictures of the contents to the outside of the box as helpful reminders. Place stacking bins in the closet, labeled "pants," "shirts," and so on. Kids can find what they need and put laundry away in a snap. Use clear vinyl shoe bags that hang over the back of a door to store easily misplaced items, bath and hair products, small toys, and Barbie dolls and their accessories. Wash and reuse baby-wipe containers for storage by removing the label and replacing it with your own. They make handy craft kits for crayons, markers, scissors, rubber stamps and ink pad, and drawer organizers for kids' socks and hair accessories. They can also be used as miniature toy chests for small blocks, action figures, and race cars. Use some in the kitchen as a caddy for sponges, steel wool scouring pads, and cleaning brushes. In the bathroom, they can be a catchall for toiletries and cosmetics.

One of the reasons we are run ragged is we don't have systems like these in place. With a little creativity and imagination, you won't have to search for a place to sit with your feet up at the end of a long day. Establishing a comfortable, well-run home can be one of the most satisfying accomplishments we moms can experience—as well as freeing up time for some well-deserved pampering pleasures!

WASH YOUR CARES AWAY

*Behind every successful woman…is a
basketful of dirty laundry.*

SALLY FORTH

y second favorite household chore is doing the laundry, the first is cleaning up an entire bag of sugar that has just dropped from the shelf and spilled into the burners of my stove. When it comes to laundry, who had the astute foresight and shrewd perception to decide that kids' baseball uniforms should be white anyway? I'm convinced it was not a mother! And this is just one of many laundry challenges moms face daily.

We all have to do laundry. It's a fact of life that isn't going away. Some of us have to face a few loads a week, while others have more than that to do nearly every day. The problem comes when we put it off until it's an overwhelming monster and we are paralyzed by the mere thought of it. How do you keep your laundry from becoming *the blob,* spreading and mushrooming throughout your house until it has jammed almost every vacant spot including the corners, chairs, and under beds? The end result is hearing your child or husband hollering, "Is the underwear in this basket the clean stuff or the dirty stuff?"

There are ways to not only get this monster under control, but to make it a pleasant experience. You might not think so, but doing the laundry can actually become a retreat in the midst of an otherwise chaotic day. Here are a few ways to take laundry time and use it to wash your cares away.

Start by making your laundry area more pleasant so you'll enjoy being in there. Spruce it up with a fresh coat of paint in a color you find comforting, or put up a pretty wallpaper border. Make it warm and homey with a little lamp tucked into a corner, a radio to play your favorite music, some framed family photos, or inspirational posters. Buy some inexpensive apothecary jars and put all your detergents and softeners in them. Add charming lace curtains, a few eye-catching knickknacks on top of a shelf, and a scented candle to burn while you are working, and you'll feel much better about spending time there. Your laundry room may even become your "quiet place."

Getting your room organized also makes laundry a more enjoyable experience. Find a multi-bin stackable laundry sorter or use a few milk crates placed on a low shelf. Show your family which bin their whites and colors go in, and have separate bins for all the towels, washcloths, and dish towels. Sorting laundry this way makes it a snap to throw in a load when you have a few minutes.

Attempting to get the laundry into the washer and dryer isn't usually the biggest problem, however. The real hitch is in the folding. Make it more interesting by having the kids bring their after-school snacks into the laundry room with you, and you can hear all about their day while you fold a load or two. If your laundry room is the basement, use the dryer cycle as a timer to see how much decluttering you can do in a particular area before the cycle ends. You'll be there to fold clothes while they are still warm or to place them on hangers so they won't need ironing. (Don't even start a load unless you intend to do this part right away.) Place folded clothes in color-coded plastic baskets for each family member to put away. You can also use an old bookcase and place each person's laundry on his own shelf.

Another option is to make folding a family affair. Sit in the living room together, pop in a good movie, and have everyone fold his or her own things. If you have toddlers, even they can learn to fold washcloths and tea towels, and they'll be proud of themselves when they take part. (Don't be too fussy, Mom!) One mother I know makes a game out of folding. Here's how it works: Player number one picks any piece to fold. Player number two must follow suit, folding something of either the same type or color. For example, navy socks mean the next person can fold socks of any color or something navy. If a player can't follow suit, they must fold two items. Of course, this works best when you have loads of both colored and white laundry to fold. It may take a few rounds for everyone to catch on, but each time you play it will get easier. Besides, you will be spending time together as a family, kids will be learning new skills, and you'll be getting an unpopular chore out of the way.

Avoid pressing problems. Wash and dry children's
clothes, then leave them in the ironing basket until the
kids outgrow them.

PEGGY GOLDTRAP

DO IT NOW

If you wait for perfect conditions,
you will never get anything done.

ECCLESIASTES 11:4 NLT

t only takes 5 minutes—to clean up a spill, sort through your mail and discard the junk, put some glasses in the dishwasher rather than the sink, make a bed, throw in a load of laundry, or fold the clothes as you take them from the dryer. Don't wait until later, when you will supposedly have more time. Here's a revelation: There isn't going to be more time! Conditions are never going to be perfect. The best time to do something is now. The longer you procrastinate, the more irritated you become. You may think you are putting things off, but your mind never lets you off the hook. Often, it takes the same amount of time and uses the same amount of energy to jump in and do something as it does to fret and grumble about it.

There are so many days when we just get overwhelmed and don't know where to start. We know what needs to be accomplished, yet we can't make ourselves pick one thing to begin with. There are so many basic tasks you can accomplish in a mere 5 minutes. For example, when you're watching television and a commercial comes on, challenge yourself to pick up as many things that are out of place in the room before the program starts up again. During the next commercial break, take those things and put them where they belong.

If you enjoy gardening but feel you don't have the time to remove weeds, you could clear one section at a time whenever you need a break from other chores. Deadhead the petunias while talking on the phone, or water the plants on your deck while you wait for supper guests to arrive. As an added benefit, getting outdoors for a few minutes can do wonders for your energy level and mood.

Challenge yourself to make this more fun. Cut some blank paper into 30 slips. On each piece, write one task that you can accomplish in 5 minutes or less—such as wash one window, purge one file folder, organize a closet, clean out a drawer, tidy one shelf in the pantry, sort through the magazines on the coffee table, clean off the top of the refrigerator, spritz and clean your mirrors with glass cleaner, and so on. Put these tasks in a container and choose one to do each day this month. Get yourself a small timer, set it for 5 minutes and when time is up, get back to what you were doing. In one month, you will have completed two-and-a-half hours worth of tasks, and it will seem as though you haven't really worked at all!

You've heard the phrase "one day at a time." Sometimes even that can be a challenge. Try 5 minutes at a time. It's usually not what we do that makes us tired as much as the mental pressure caused by what we put off doing. Pick one thing and do it now!

PART 6

SILENCE, STILLNESS, AND SOLITUDE

THE SILENT TREATMENT

Silence...a healing for all ailments.

HEBREW PROVERB

t's almost certain that at least once in recent years you've caught yourself saying in typical *mother* fashion: "It's so noisy around here I can't hear myself think," or "if only I had a little peace and quiet." The old saying is true: Silence *is* golden. These days, it's a rare commodity for moms, not just because of fussy babies, Power Rangers, Sesame Street, toddler temper tantrums, and V-Tech toys, but because we forget the purpose of silence and neglect to chase after it.

Somewhere along the line, we started equating quietness with emptiness and solitude with loneliness. I've even had women tell me they find silence frightening. Somehow, we have bought into the idea that we are forever supposed to be talking with or listening to someone. If we're not, we wish we could be. A friend of mine recently shared with a group of other moms that the night before, she sat in a coffee shop, ordered a cappuccino, and read a book—alone. Her friends responded with *oohs* and *aahs* of reverence and respect, impressed that she went by herself, but more amazed she didn't talk to anyone while she was there.

When you are feeling irritable and you know it's because of the noise around you, try this experiment. Periodically during the day, stop what you are doing, seek out the most quiet spot you can find, and for 5 minutes focus on the silence. Whether you choose a sunny corner of a cozy room, a spot in the garden, or like some of us, a closet or the basement, your goal is not to be aware of your surroundings, but to allow a sense of immense quiet to gently enfold you.

Years ago when my children were toddlers, I found quiet time by setting the alarm to go off at 5 A.M. I could have two silent hours before the house became filled with sounds of Mr. Dress Up, the telephone ringing, and sibling squabbles. At that hour, the house was quiet, the dog was still asleep, and it was delightfully peaceful. You may not need two whole hours. Some moms are able to fill their quota with an uninterrupted 5-minute shower, by turning off the television a few minutes early each evening, or by simply making the pursuit of personal quiet time a priority throughout the day.

We have grown so accustomed to noise it sometimes seems as though silence could swallow us up. On those rare occasions when no one is talking or we're home alone, we have the tendency to fill the hush with background noise. We turn on the TV, pop in a video, or put on a CD. Don't be afraid. Once you become at ease with silence, you will learn the influence that quiet time can have in your life. Silence is a restorative hiatus in a busy day, a pause made all the more striking against the usual clamor and commotion of motherhood. A bit of quietness in your day will help you appreciate and even welcome the noise of family that will inevitably return! Try weaving some silence into your day. You might just grow to treasure quiet times to reflect, think, contemplate, pray, and listen to the voice of God.

A SANCTUARY
OF STILLNESS

*Teach me the art of creating islands of
stillness, in which I can absorb the
beauty of everyday things.*

MARIAN STROUD

In days gone by, when friends ran into each other and asked, "How are you?" the answer was invariably, "Fine, thank you. And you?" Today, the response is more likely to be, "I am so busy. I'm always on the run. I just wish I had more time," or "I can't seem to get caught up. If only there were more hours in a day." These are usually followed by apologies for not being able to get together along with vows to have coffee and catch up once life settles down.

Most of us are too busy. We are always on the move and spend our days literally "running" errands. We attempt to cram far too much into too little time. As moms, we juggle home, work, family, friends, and volunteer activities, and we're good at it. On an average day, aside from packing lunches, getting kids off to school, tidying the house, swishing the toilet, throwing in a load of laundry, and putting something in the slow cooker for dinner, we're also picking up parcels at the post office, dropping off clothes to be dry-cleaned, taking shoes to be repaired, stopping at the market, and going to the library to do research for a work project. What we're not good at is being still. Tim Himmel, author of *Little House on the Freeway*, says, "We have a love affair with haste. We call it convenience, and there is no doubt that many modern conveniences have made some of the mundane duties of life more tolerable. But there is a subtle programming that goes on at the same time. It's not long before we drive our lives the way we drive our cars—too fast."

Imagine how different your life would be if you created 5-minute islands of stillness during your day. At the very least, you may have a chance to absorb the beauty of everyday things. At the most, you may reclaim your life with renewed vision. Ponder the word *stillness*. When I looked it up in the thesaurus, I found words like tranquil, calm, serene, composed, unruffled, unflustered, unflappable, and unperturbed. It made me realize there really isn't much stillness in a typical day for many moms. The opposite is more like it—to live in a state of commotion and flurry, to feel agitated, restless, frantic, frenzied, or harried.

How much better we would feel if we would slow down and pause in our full schedules to catch our breath, to get lost in the moment, to appreciate the miraculous. Our heavenly Father says, "Be still and know that I am God." He knows that we also need to experience stillness in order to create an environment of serenity and peace for our families to return to at the end of a day.

For 5 minutes at a time, consciously choose to move in a slow, unhurried, laid-back pace. Purposely slow yourself down when you eat, drive, walk, and talk. Eliminate the phrase "I'm too busy" from your vocabulary, which implies something outside yourself is in control of your time. Say instead, "I have a full schedule" and put yourself back in charge.

SWEET SOLITUDE

Solitude...a divine retreat.

EDWARD YOUNG

n a letter I received recently, a young mom wrote, "Last month, I did something I've never done before. The kids stayed with friends for the weekend, Dad stayed home, and I took off to the country (less than an hour away). I stayed at an inn and just sat and thought. You wouldn't believe how much good it did me!" You may find the thought of this retreat alluring, even tempting, and not self-indulgent in the least! Privacy, isolation, and seclusion may seem like foreign words to you, especially if you have little people following you from room to room, and the bathroom is the only guilt-free refuge you have. Even there, tiny hands may pound on the other side of a locked door, jockeying for your attention. Or, bigger hands are letting you know they are waiting in line for their turn in the sanctuary as well.

Times of absolute quiet, spent alone, with space to yourself, are extremely essential factors in maintaining your sanity. Moments where you are briefly unaffected by others' wants and needs are vital in helping you alleviate burnout and breakdown. Without respites, you're headed for certain collapse. Eventually, you will feel fragmented, as though parts of you have been strewn all over the universe. You might be saying, "Yes, I know it's crucial for me to take time for myself, but it's just not possible to get away for a personal hideaway. Even if I had my very own sanctuary, I have too many responsibilities and people counting on me." Think of learning to spend time alone as a skill that can be acquired and enhanced—one that is well worth obtaining and refining.

At some point today, take some time to sit quietly with a journal and write these words: solitude, alone, privacy, seclusion, solitary, and isolation. Explore them and get to know what they represent to you. Ponder them during the rest of the day. What images come to mind that represent solitary time and a peaceful place? Then list 10 things about solitude—what you like and appreciate, what you dislike or can't bear. Sometimes we may be afraid to be alone for too long. When we take time to know ourselves, to look inside, we fear we may not like what we find. Then, we keep ourselves too busy on purpose because it's easier. Guilt often holds us back. Fear and guilt are traps we fall prey to, and the only way to free ourselves is to face them head on.

In other cases, it's too easy to blame our lack of solitude on our situation or others, such as our children, jobs, or spouses. If we want to move from a victim position to a more powerful stance, it's time to take responsibility. Say quietly, "I take full responsibility for how I choose to spend my time." Then ask yourself how your life would be different if you had time that was undisturbed and uninterrupted. What benefits would you experience? Would you be more pleasant to live with, have increased energy, or love and appreciate your family more? It's been said that if we can come up with enough reasons why we want to do something, we will always find a way! Give yourself permission to experience solitude. Be gentle with yourself. It may take practice, but the rewards are priceless.

PEACEFUL
INTERLUDES

*It is a good thing to let prayer be the
first business of the morning and
the last of the evening.*

MARTIN LUTHER

irst thing in the morning and last thing at night are perfect opportunities for 5-minute retreats. Book-ending your day with peace means providing a quiet and serene interlude for your spirit when you first awaken and again in those few moments before drifting off to sleep at night. What is an interlude? It's a pause, a break in the normal flow of things, providing a time for introspection, reflective thought, and pensive meditation. A peaceful interlude happens when you choose to suspend all that you are doing or thinking, and take a temporary hiatus from the cares of the day. It's a breather, a respite, a time to linger, to lift up your heart to the Father and ask Him to take charge of your life today and every day. Use those few moments to pray, meditate, and read Scripture or a passage from an inspirational book. Contemplate the next day and the ways it might evolve more smoothly. Envision yourself moving through your day's events with ease and comfort. In your mind's eye, see yourself as productive and stress-free, enjoying well-deserved periods of peace throughout the day. Visualize orderliness and harmony within your home and family, rather than the mayhem, disarray, or confusion that might have been part of the day before.

When you read this suggestion to invest a little time for yourself, it may seem impossible. By the time you climb the stairs to your bedroom at night, you may feel as though you could fall asleep standing up, and when the alarm goes off in the morning, it sometimes seems as though you are more weary and worn out than when you went to bed. You may be thinking, "Here's a woman who doesn't understand what I deal with on a daily basis or have a clue how exhausting my life really is!" Yet by rousing yourself from bed a few minutes before anyone else is up, and staying up for a bit after everyone else has settled in to experience that peaceful interlude, you will discover you are able to live in this world but not be caught up in the turmoil of it, especially when some of the turmoil is of your own doing.

Just before drifting off to sleep, ask God to direct your tomorrows. When you awake, snuggle under the covers and embrace the sacredness of the moment. Occasionally take a cup of coffee and meander out into the garden early in the morning, or sit on the back porch and wait for the sun to rise. Notice how nature and time rush for no one. One hand on the clock does not tell the other, "Hurry up—there are lunches to be packed, appointments to be kept, laundry to be done, groceries to be picked up." There are and always will be 24 hours in a day. We will never have more time. Your frazzled soul is crying out for some peace and harmony. It all starts within as you begin and end each day with prayer and quiet reflection.

DOODLE YOUR DOLDRUMS AWAY

Some carefree people do their best thinking on paper.

Remember rainy Saturdays when you were a child? You could spend hours at the kitchen table with a box full of art supplies and craft projects. There were cut-out dolls you could dress in enviable fashions from elegant balls to horseback riding. There was an assortment of coloring books along with a tin of well-worn crayons—some fluorescent, most broken and missing their wrappers—and sheets of colorful construction paper with child-sized scissors, tape, and a bottle of glue. There was a big box with watercolors and a single brush, a pad of art paper, jars of finger paint in primary colors, pencil crayons, a small plastic sharpener, a pink eraser, a wooden ruler, stencils, and some modeling clay, which eventually turned into a marbled ball of indistinguishable shades. Left to your boundless imagination, it didn't take long to become immersed in creativity and oblivious to the passing of time.

Wouldn't it be fun to do it again? Try to recapture the freedom of expressing yourself with total abandon. Without all your adult inhibitions, spend a few minutes doodling and dabbling to your heart's content. Allow your pent-up emotions to flow down your arm and out of your body through your pencil or pen. Get an artist's hardcover sketchbook, a blank notepad, or a 3-ring binder filled with drawing paper (borrow some from your children!), and create a personal wellspring of comfort you can return to whenever you feel the need for respite. Gather some art supplies and get lost in your imagination. Draw, paste, sketch, or paint images that portray contentment and relaxation for you. Make this retreat a safe haven by including anything that makes you feel free, playful, peaceful, or secure. Find a spot where you will be undisturbed to unwind and loosen up. Then, immerse yourself in the experience.

Fill a pretty basket, an eye-catching floral hatbox, or a delightful wicker chest with supplies that will spark your imagination and ignite your creativity. Start a collection of colored markers, pens and pencils, paints, glue, glitter, and a brand-new box of Crayola crayons. Collect feathers, fabric scraps, felt, yarn, ribbon, seashells, string, confetti, bits of decorative foil, and leaves or flowers you have pressed. Include leftover wallpaper, gift wrap, and shelf paper. You'll be all set to tap your creativity if you need to take a break or when the mood strikes.

We have convinced ourselves that we can't possibly squeeze time for personal pursuits into our schedules for the sole purpose of nurturing creativity. We are too practical to be passionate about the inner longings. However, we need to recapture that part of us. When you become passionate and fervent about carving out the time it takes, when you start to respect the creative woman inside you who yearns to draw, paint, sketch, or simply doodle and dawdle, you will discover delight in the mundane and spiritual fulfillment in all you create.

YOU CAN'T DO
IT ALONE

Charity begins at home.

TERENCE

e often get so caught up in our needs of the moment that we overlook the fact there is help available. There are able bodies and capable hands right under our noses. In most cases, our spouses, kids, parents, and even neighbors would come to our rescue if they knew how much we needed them. Our job is to get better at asking for assistance, discover creative ways to delegate certain tasks, and learn to hire help when necessary. A good starting place is to let go of the belief you can do it all or you can do it alone.

In days gone by, families lived together or at least in close proximity. When I was growing up, Grandpa was available to come over and do some home repairs, and occasionally take us kids for an ice cream cone so Mom could have a break. Grandma did not have a career outside the home, so she was there to be a role model and mentor, helping out with the children and some chores.

Today, with the absence of the extended family, most moms face each day on their own, balancing the stresses of motherhood and a career. And many still find it difficult to ask for assistance, delegate tasks, or pay for help. When you are tempted to do it alone, ask yourself, "Is this the best use of my time?" One of the most difficult things I had to do in my home was hire a cleaning lady, because I actually enjoy the satisfaction I get from cleaning my own home. But when I asked myself the above question, the answer was no. I now know my time can be spent in more productive and beneficial ways because I hire help.

Even when we do grant ourselves permission to ask our spouses, parents, or neighbors for help or hire it when it's needed, we don't always think to enlist our children to help. Having your kids help out around the house is beneficial in many ways. Not only does it help you get your work completed, but it also makes them feel like contributing members of the household.

But how much of a retreat can having little kids help around the house realistically provide for you? Not much, to be honest! But sometimes just enough to help you get the job done, or at the very least, to keep them occupied so they won't be whining or squabbling. A two year old can help unload clothing from the dryer and put clean clothes away, a four year old can take out the garbage, and older children can dust, vacuum, and feed or walk the dog. When you enlist the help of a young child, be sure the task you assign is age-appropriate and the job is small enough for your child to accomplish, since not being able to complete the task can actually backfire by undermining the child's self-esteem. Kids thrive on positive reinforcement, so be sure to acknowledge the good job they've done!

A SENSE OF SATISFACTION

*The ordinary acts we practice every day at
home are of more importance to the soul than
their simplicity might suggest.*

THOMAS MOORE

f your day has been one of dashing to the grocery store
with tired, hungry kids in tow, arriving at home to start
dinner amid overwhelming bedlam, only to find the
family has run out of clean clothes to wear and the dishwasher is full
of dirty dishes, embarking on one more task may not be what you
had in mind to get away from it all!

Certain tasks *can* be a retreat if they're things you enjoy doing. An
activity you can carry out from start to finish, and one that offers a
sense of completion is a rare commodity these days since most of our
daily projects tend to blend into each other.

My sister and I, who both have offices at home, were discussing
ways we deal with the stress of work overload. Amazingly we both
had the same remedy—get into the kitchen and bake a dozen
muffins. We've both found there are many benefits of baking. It's
something that can be done in just a few minutes, takes your mind
temporarily away from what is causing the stress, and provides a
sense of achievement. There is a beginning and an end. You can
make this even more appealing by using one of the convenient and
tasty mixes available on the market today. Simply add a variety of
nuts, seeds, raisins, and dates to make the recipe your own.

A retreat task is one that provides a few moments of quiet contemplation and reflection amid the hustle and bustle of a busy household. At one time, these opportunities were present in the mere nature of our daily tasks. While hanging clothes on the line, we enjoyed the warmth of sunshine on our faces, listened to the song of a bird nearby, and felt a cool breeze on our skin. While ironing, baking bread, or preparing a kettle of stew, we had time to think our own thoughts, dream about our future, and plan our goals. Washing dishes by hand gave us time to ponder the truths of life, listen to the voice of God, and discover the divine wisdom we need to make the best choices. Today, with all our modern conveniences (not that I'd opt to do without them!), we simply don't have the same opportunities for silent reflection. Instead we must seek out new opportunities for quiet contemplation. Today, choose to do one simple 5-minute task that will nurture your soul and restore a sense of balance to your life.

CURL UP
FOR A NAP

No day is so bad it can't be
fixed with a nap.

CARRIE SNOW

here's a mother's prayer that goes something like this: "Dear Lord, this day has been great so far, and I have so much to be thankful for. Up until now, no one has thrown any hissy fits (including me), no one has spilled their Cinnamon Crunch cereal all over the clean floor, I haven't said anything I will regret, the toilet hasn't overflowed, I haven't eaten anything that will go straight to my hips, I haven't allowed myself to think or say anything negative about anyone, and I haven't missed my exercise class. But Lord, the alarm clock just went off, and it's almost time to get out of bed. Then I'm really going to need your help!"

Sometimes the nicest, safest, coziest retreat in the world is in your bed. Although you know you can't stay there forever (well, you could, but after a week or so, some nice people in white coats would take you away and check you into an institution), there are times when you will want to retreat to your safe haven. Moms can use afternoon naps now and then, too. We really shouldn't feel guilty if we'd consider that taking a midday snooze is a natural, intrinsic behavior. It's one of the last things we abandon in our infancy and one of the first we resume as seniors. It's a built-in part of our natural human rhythm yet, during the in-between years, we have bought into the idea it's not necessary. We know our children need recess and other cultures have siestas. Even machinery needs down time, and fields need to be left uncultivated for a season. However, we think we can go on all day without taking a few minutes to close our eyes and recover.

How do you snooze when you have children? Simple—you nap when they nap or when they're in school! I can hear you saying, "But that's when I catch up on all the work that needs to be done." Well, you will get a lot more done in less time once you develop the habit of taking catnaps in the middle of the day. You will go back to those chores with more energy and creative problem-solving ideas. Once you realize the benefits of napping, you'll make it a priority.

Ease yourself into napping with a Sunday afternoon snooze. While supper is in the oven, slip away and crawl under the covers. Let the family know you have something important to attend to (what could be more important that catching a few winks?), and you'll be back in a few minutes. Then, crawl right under the covers, snuggle up with a plump pillow, and allow yourself to doze off without guilt.

Whether you nap in a chair in front of a blazing fire, a chaise lounge in the garden, a hammock under a shade tree, or in bed under the covers, develop the habit of regularly drifting off for a few minutes. When you do, you will handle the challenges of the rest of the day with ease and a greatly improved sense of humor.

Don't confuse snoozing with sleeping. When we sleep, we do so because our physical bodies need rejuvenating. A nap restores the soul, and is as refreshing as rain to a fading rose.

SERENITY 101

The day is always his, who works in it with
serenity and great aims.

RALPH WALDO EMERSON

erenity—what a pleasant word. To be tranquil, calm, peaceful, and still. If you're like most moms, serenity is not a familiar state. Let's face it. In order to feel serene, you need to have some time to yourself. And to work that into your day, you almost have to take a course—Serenity 101.

Let's say you do have a few minutes to spare. (I know you don't, so just pretend.) How would you spend your leftover moments? Would you zip through the house picking up stray shoes, coffee mugs, juice glasses, socks, pizza boxes, newspapers, and junk mail on your way to throw in a load of laundry? Would you partially make the bed, but then interrupt yourself to add something to your to-do list in the kitchen, and while you're there, start cleaning the counters and forget about the bed altogether? I used to tear through the house while foaming at the mouth because of all the things I remembered I wanted to do right in the middle of brushing my teeth! Maybe in your spare minutes you would make a steamy cup of tea, curl up in a comfy chair, put your feet up, and browse through your favorite magazine that just arrived in the mail. If so, good for you! You are the exception. Many of us are so unaccustomed to having time to ourselves we would probably seize up and then fritter away our time gazing into the distance, not knowing how to spend it. This is not what serenity is all about.

It is so rare that moms get to be alone in a quiet house, with all the kids either occupied or away at the same time, the mere thought of such a possibility almost overwhelms us. When you find yourself becoming overly ecstatic and extremely euphoric at the mere chance of experiencing solitude and serenity (You'll know your reaction is dreadfully out of proportion when you realize you're doing cartwheels in the living room while singing "Oh, Happy Day!"), see it as a signal that you are overdue for some serenity time.

Recognizing that you deserve time for yourself is only the beginning. The answer is to plan to have serenity retreats regularly and practice them without the guilt complex. Stop listening to your inner critic and let go of concerns about what others would think. Give yourself the attention and effort you already lavish on your family. Create some daily serenity habits—applying a deliciously scented body lotion first thing each morning; placing a bouquet of fresh flowers on your table every Monday (just because); taking a morning stroll, an afternoon nap, or an evening bubble bath; making a nightly routine of writing in your journal; or lighting candles and playing soft music while you do household chores.

You need a steady diet of serenity moments. If you rely on chance to find them, they come along too seldom or not at all. Motherhood is a special calling, and one that most certainly involves a lot of self-sacrifice. But when being a mom becomes so all-consuming that you end up exhausted, bored, and empty, you have nothing left to offer those you live with. That's why we need to be true to ourselves. So for a few moments, shut off the phone, half-ignore the kids, totally ignore the housework, and give yourself the gift of enrolling in a class—Serenity 101.

WHEN MOM IS SICK

Do what it says on the aspirin bottle: Take 2 tablets. Keep away from children.

irst of all, moms aren't supposed to get sick. It's not included in the job description. You might be able to get away with grumpy, grouchy, or down in the dumps, even snappy, crabby, absent-minded, or behind schedule, but sick is something that just doesn't register. Your family cannot quite figure out how to deal with a mom who's not able-bodied.

Kids tend to think of Mom in the same way they do hot water, electricity, television, food on the table, and milk in the refrigerator. She's just *there*, that is, until she's feeling under the weather. Meals still need to be prepared, groceries have to be replenished, and clothes need to be washed. There are errands to be run, fights to be refereed, science fair projects to be supervised, and advice to be doled out—requested and otherwise.

Mom does not have time to be sick. Even if Dad is around, it's usually Mom who knows about car-pool schedules, guitar lessons, favorite foods, soccer practice, and dental appointments. Dad is vaguely aware of some short people living in the house. So how does a mom respond when all she can do is muster enough energy to say, "Indoor voices only, please."

Here's what you do: You start to practice *healthy selfishness* and put your own needs first—a drastic step for most moms. We'll call the doctor in an instant for kids with fevers, bumps on the head, and bloody noses. But when it comes to us, it's easier to take something for the pain and do our best to carry on as usual. Taking care of you means just that. You cut back, limit yourself, decrease your work-load, and curb your natural inclination to keep going despite the fact that you are white as a ghost, burning with fever, and shaking like a leaf. How you ask? You do only what cannot be left undone. Ask yourself a few questions to determine if the situation is a crisis and needs your personal attention. If this doesn't get done, will the house burn down? Will someone be injured? Can it be delegated or ignored? Can it be done by anyone else? The answers to those ques-tions will be guides as to what you will and won't do while you recover.

Don't make yourself worse by giving in to the most hard-hitting symptom of all: guilt. You'll recognize it when you start saying "I should..." ("I should get up and get dressed." "I should make some-thing nice for dinner." "I should make an effort to be more agree-able.") When you catch yourself saying you *should* do anything, the first question to ask is "Why?" Then, "Says who?" If you can't come up with a good reason, lay your aching head back on that pillow and stay put until you know you're good and ready to get going again. It's not such a bad idea for your kids to see you sick. It helps them rec-ognize you are not just the laundry-doing, supper-cooking, lunch-packing, car-pooling device they're accustomed to.

Allow your children to nurture you. They have an infinite supply of genuine compassion. They can fluff your pillows, brush your hair, and tuck you in. A toddler may want to snuggle and nap with you under the covers. Turn on the television, let them eat arrowroot bis-cuits, and ask for all the help you can rally. When you remind your-self that in a few days this will be just a memory, you may want to enjoy your comfy couch and cozy quilt a little more, and linger in your frailty for a bit longer!

What matters is that one be, for a time, inwardly attentive.

ANNE MORROW LINDBERGH

174

TEA FOR ME
WITH TLC

I had a little tea party this afternoon at three,
T'was very small—three guests in all, just I,
myself, and me. Myself ate all the sandwiches,
while I drank up the tea. T'was also I who ate the
pie, and passed the cake to me.

AUTHOR UNKNOWN

here's an ancient Chinese proverb that says, "Better to be deprived of food for three days than tea for one." My sentiments exactly! It's been said drinking tea is a comforting ritual—simultaneously soothing and stimulating—that allows us to briefly retreat from the busyness of our lives. When I'm feeling run-down and want to withdraw momentarily from the world, all I really need is a few deep breaths, the view from my kitchen window, and a steamy cup of tea in my hands. The mere thought of it brings the anticipation of a few moments of peace and tranquility. When you are so burned out you can barely keep going, or you're simply craving some private space, find a moment in your hectic schedule to treat yourself to a teatime. The tradition of tea has the remarkable ability to satisfy our yearning for quiet serenity and inner contentment. Sipping tea restores balance and harmony in our lives.

It doesn't take much to turn this brief respite from the world into a royal ceremony. Pamper yourself by drinking tea from your very best mug, or in a pretty china cup and saucer—the ones you normally reserve for company! It's no faster or easier to have tea in your old mug with the chip and stains on the inside. You'll feel much better about your special time when you use the best.

Go all out and prepare an attractive tea tray for yourself. Spoil yourself with all your favorite things—a beautiful lace cloth, a pretty linen napkin, a tiny vase of fresh flowers, some tea biscuits, a muffin, or a few slices of buttered nut bread. A treat for me is an Empire biscuit from our local bakery, or fresh-baked orange-pecan muffins topped with honey butter, but animal crackers and arrowroot biscuits work just fine, too! Use your best china teapot and brew your tea the old-fashioned way. Warm the pot with boiling water, then add your preferred blend of tea and let it steep for 5 minutes. Light a cinnamon-scented candle and add some soft background music. Grab a beloved book, curl up in a rocking chair with a cozy quilt, and retreat from the world for at least 5 minutes. Linger over the moment. Enjoy the space and the break from routine. For a few moments, you will feel truly blessed and nurtured, and when the time is up, you'll be prepared to face the world again.

Certain teas provide particular benefits. Fruit and spice teas can energize, peppermint tea settles an upset tummy, lavender tea pacifies us when we're out of sorts, and chamomile acts as a completely natural sedative, making it an ideal bedtime tea—both the aroma and the flavor help lull you to sleep. Children can enjoy drinking tea, too. While you won't want them drinking beverages with caffeine, herbal teas are both tasty and healthy. Choose from many varieties they might enjoy, including orange spice, apple and cinnamon, almond, cranberry, or lemon.

With the ever-increasing complexities of being a mom, a wife, and a homemaker, it's no wonder you long for and cherish times of tranquility and comfort. So, go now and brew a pot of tea...unwind, calm down, lighten up, and let go.

QUIET MOMENTS

We need to find God, and He cannot be
found in noise and restlessness.
God is the friend of silence.

MOTHER TERESA

ry to remember the last time you had 5 minutes of complete and utter quiet. It has probably been a while. Our days are generally filled with noise. First thing, they start off with the nerve-jangling shriek of the alarm clock, or maybe at your house, it's the nerve-jangling shriek of a newborn baby. Then comes the roaring blast of hair dryers, the hum of electric toothbrushes, and the blare of the television. Once the kids are up, they're hollering—at each other, at whomever is taking too long in the bathroom, or at the school bus that just left without them. The dog is growling to alert you to the fact the postman has dared to tread on your property—again. Outside, there's the ear-shattering roar of the neighbor's lawn mower, leaf blower, or snow plow, depending on the season. Living in a noisy world can be stressful—whether we're aware of it or not.

Moments of quiet and calmness act as wonderful counterbalances to the action and activity in our homes that can throw off our equilibrium. We all need times of absolute quiet for a number of reasons, including to stay focused and to be more creative problem-solvers. Planning intervals of quiet, as much as possible in your own space, is a necessity. Waiting and hoping for it to happen just won't work.

Make some conscious choices regarding noise control. When you are in your car, you don't have to listen to the radio all the time. Occasionally, shut it off. Ask yourself, just for today, if you can do without hearing the latest news report or talk show you tune in to every morning. If you are home alone, resist the urge to turn on the TV or radio for background noise. Manage the telephone. Remind yourself that it works for you, not the other way around. The phone has become the master rather than the servant it was designed to be. Let the machine pick up calls, especially during heart-to-heart family talks, intimate moments, or meals—a favorite time for telemarketers to call. You can listen to messages at your convenience. If you find the phone hard to ignore, turn down the ringer so you won't know someone's trying to reach you.

Look at your calendar and actually schedule breaks. Try to keep one or two mornings or evenings free each week. You can use this time to catch up if you want or need to. This way, you'll be prepared and organized in your other commitments during the week. If you want to use the time for a mental pause, to simply sit in stillness and serenity, to collect your thoughts, or to mediate and pray, your quiet moments will better equip you for hectic times to come.

When you're working on projects that require absolute quiet, get the family to take you seriously by labeling your time "The Silent Hour," or "Mom's Quiet Zone." They'll have a better understanding that it's your time—alone. You need that sacred time and place where you won't be disturbed.

My most valuable quiet moments are when I get outdoors to go for a walk. I've tried walking with girlfriends, because I believed it was a good way to make exercise more pleasant, but we'd end up having a good old gabfest at the same time. As much as I enjoyed that, I found I missed the quiet. I came to realize it wasn't the exercise I was craving as much as a time of silence. Now, I separate exercising with friends from walking when I need quiet time. "There should be, even in the busiest day," Christian author Caryll Houselander reminds us, "a few moments when we can close our eyes and let God possess us." Do yourself a favor—instead of waiting for it to happen, make it happen.

PART 7

FAMILY, FRIENDS, AND FUN

LET THE
GAMES BEGIN!

Oh, the fun of arriving at a house and feeling
the spark that tells you that you are going
to have a good time!

MARK HAMPTON

Whenever we are invited to the homes of particular friends, we know that we are in for a lot of fun and laughter because playing games is sure to be a big part of the evening. When our children were growing up, playing a game of Yahtzee, Crazy Eights, Monopoly, or Charades was always a popular Saturday night treat. Today, board games are popular again. Families are recognizing the benefits of an old-fashioned game night. Playing together offers a chance to interact with each other and see children's personality traits emerge that might not be seen at any other time. Seek out games that require little effort and everyone can enjoy. Playing in teams is a way of softening the competitive aspect. At least when you are on the losing team, you're all in it together!

Get creative in planning snacks for your game night, especially if it's going to be a party atmosphere. Aside from a big basket of hot buttered popcorn, try making fun and simple snacks. For an appetizer, make a cream cheese cracker spread in the shape of a large domino. Blend cream cheese, shredded mozzarella, minced onion, and Worcestershire sauce. Press the mixture into a loaf pan lined with plastic wrap. Refrigerate the loaf overnight, then remove it from the pan, peel away the plastic wrap, and place it on a platter. Blend a little more cream cheese with a teaspoon of milk to spread over top and sides of the slab. Finally, arrange pitted black-olive halves on the top to resemble the markings on a domino! Serve it with a variety of chips and crackers.

Another idea is to make edible game chips out of red, green, and yellow bell peppers by using a small round cookie cutter. Cut circles from the peppers and stack or scatter them on a platter to be served with sour cream vegetable dip. For dessert, make Scrabble squares. Start with blonde brownies iced with chocolate frosting and cut in squares. With a tube of vanilla frosting, write one letter on each square. Position several on a serving platter to form words in the shape of a Scrabble game.

When decorating, old playing cards become coasters for your drinks and they can also be used as invitations, with printed information and all the details glued to the decorative side. Cover the table with a white paper tablecloth and use crayons to draw tic-tac-toe games. Guests can play in between rounds or while waiting for snacks to be served. For a simple centerpiece, toss game markers or dice around a vase of flowers. Scatter gold foil-wrapped coins over the table for added flair or munching.

When there are only two of you, remember to get out the old reliables: backgammon, dominoes, checkers, Scrabble, and cribbage. And here's a good rule of thumb for any game night: Show extreme humility when you win and extreme dignity when you lose. Boastful winners and sore losers—in games and in life—are rarely respected by anyone!

LAUGHING MATTERS

*Laughter is a corrective force, which prevents us
from becoming cranks.*

HENRI BERGSON

ur granddaughter Cassie, even as a toddler, is already displaying a delightful sense of humor. She'll occasionally say, "Grandma Sue, let's laugh!" and we proceed to force ourselves to chuckle until it turns into uproarious giggling, eventually progressing into side-splitting laughter. Soon everyone within earshot joins in uncontrollably because that kind of laughter is so contagious. Then, out of the blue, Cassie stops abruptly, screws up her face and asks quite seriously, "What's so funny, Grandma?" Of course, this starts the laughter all over again!

Did you know you can actually make yourself laugh any time you choose? It might not be easy, especially if you're not in the habit of laughing regularly. After all, with the many responsibilities moms have—persuading kids to eat at least one thing in their lifetime that is green and leafy; pleading with them to remove dirty socks and underwear from beneath their beds; reminding them they can't fool you because you have eyes in the back of your head; insisting they close the front door because you can't afford to heat the whole neighborhood; convincing them the basket of folded clean clothes at the bottom of the stairs is meant to go upstairs at some point; and requesting that they stop using their sleeve for a handkerchief, to name a few—it's not surprising that laughter doesn't come easily.

It's estimated our children laugh on average 500 times a day. In contrast, moms only laugh about half a dozen times in 24 hours. And that means genuine laughter, not the hysterical, out-of-control variety that ends in giant, inconsolable sobs as you lay in a heap on the just-mopped kitchen floor now covered in some unrecognizable sticky substance. In other words, we mothers have a long way to go in order to meet our daily laughter quotient.

The family that laughs together won't easily be destroyed by typical family plagues—like the terrible twos or teens. So try this: Every day for the next week, spend 5 minutes laughing, preferably alone (adults may want to commit you to an institution otherwise!) or with the kids. (I guarantee they'll join in without much prompting.) You may have to fake it to get started...or maybe even all the way through. Someone referred to this as the habit of "acting as if" you were ecstatic. It's also been referred to as "fake it till you make it." Imagine you're an actor, auditioning for a laughing part. Eventually, true laughter does take over. If necessary, have the children tickle your feet until it drives you crazy! Laugh so hard you cry. A good, hearty 5-minute laugh helps you feel better and stay healthier. As the Bible reminds us, "A cheerful heart does good like medicine."

CREATE A HUMOR SURVIVAL KIT

*A good laugh is as good as
a prayer sometimes.*

L.M. MONTGOMERY

here are going to be days when laughing is the last thing you feel like doing—when your back aches, there's nothing for supper, it's been ages since you had your hair styled, you're close to burnout, you feel like an irritated junkyard dog, and you think nothing will ever seem funny again. Be ready for those times and purposely integrate humor into your life by having a stress-relief laughter kit handy. Fill it with some playful props—bubbles and an assortment of wands, Groucho or pop-out eyeglasses, a red clown nose, plastic animal noses, paper masks of celebrities, a feather boa, and a collection of funny hats and wigs. Get them out and wear them whenever you're about to snap someone's head off or you can't remember when you laughed till you cried. I like to have a magic wand handy for those times when people make unrealistic demands. I can pull it out, wave it back and forth, and say, "Your wish is granted!" Then ask if they'd like fries with that order. One woman told me she has a button in her humor kit that reads, "Stop me! I'm becoming my mother." Once you're on the lookout for props, there will be no end to what you will find.

Cheer up your environment while you're at it. Hang a bulletin board in plain view and plaster it with posters, funny cartoons, jokes, riddles, quotes, greeting cards, and bumper stickers—anything that will bring a smile or make you chuckle. Strategically place funny pictures where you keep your cleaning supplies. I have a picture of a man sitting on a ride-on mower as if he is vacuuming the living room. The caption reads, "If men did housework!" Put your favorite comic strips or photos of loved ones—adorable baby pictures, humorous vacation snapshots, amusing birthday photos, comical pet moments—near the washer and dryer, ironing board, broom closet, and desk where you pay bills. They'll at least bring a smile while you do something you find less than pleasant.

Start your own library of humorous books, videos, audiotapes, and CDs that will kick start your funny bone. Arrange them on a separate shelf apart from other books and tapes so that you can put your hands on them instantly. When you need a 5-minute humor retreat, you won't waste any time searching. Keep some comedy cassettes in your car for times when you are stuck in traffic or running behind schedule. You may even bring a smile to other drivers when they see you laughing hysterically.

Memorize a really good, but clean, joke and tell it to at least five people during the week. Print out lists of funny quotes, sayings, and one-liners, and place them in a special humor file. Read them at the dinner table or let the kids take turns gathering and reading their own.

Don't wait for laughter to happen. Incorporate humor into your life. It's been said that laughter is like jogging on the inside. In that case, the best form of aerobics must be belly laughing!

SMILE AT SOMEONE

What sunshine is to flowers,
a smile is to humanity

JOSEPH ADDISON

t's been said there are hundreds of languages in the world, but a smile speaks them all. Have you ever noticed how grateful—and responsive—most people are when you're the first one to reach out with a smile? Sometimes they might appear to be a little taken aback, because friendly glances, especially those with direct eye contact, have become scarce and unexpected in our society. For one full day, try to smile more than usual. Smile at your children, your spouse, a neighbor, the mail lady. Make it bigger and brighter than ever before. Choose to smile at more people than you would normally—babies, seniors, store clerks, bank tellers, and waitresses. Because smiles are contagious, you won't be the only one smiling for long. "A smile is the shortest distance between two people," said Victor Borge.

"Put on a happy face" is more than an amusing expression. It's a known fact that the muscles you use to smile send messages to the brain, releasing endorphins, some of which are more powerful than morphine, into the bloodstream. Not only do you actually begin to feel better and more optimistic about your situation, any physical pain you are experiencing can also be relieved. I know people who use a smile for all types of pain—headache, back pain, sore shoulders, stiff neck—and they vow it works. If you have a different kind of "pain in the neck" upsetting your world today, try smiling. You'll at least have him or her wondering what you're up to!

For some added fun, have the kids make you a "smile on a stick!" In fact, have them make a whole variety. Cut out an assortment of silly, giant smiles—all shapes and sizes—from cardboard or construction paper. With glue, crayons, paints, colored markers, and glitter, have the children decorate their smiles, complete with lips and teeth. Encourage them to use their imaginations and get creative. Attach each one with glue to the top of a Popsicle stick so they can hold up their "smiles" in front of their own, or secure them with rubber bands to wear as a "smile mask." Keep them handy, and when the kids can tell you just can't muster one of your own, they can put on a happy face for you or give you one of theirs. These smiles also work to cheer up a sick friend, a grouchy spouse, or anyone who needs a *face* lift! Include them in your correspondence, use them as greeting cards, or place them in flower arrangements. Keep some in the car, too! The kids can also make a few grumpy versions for those times when a smile just isn't coming. It'll be a good reminder to lighten up when tension is high and family members are ready to snap at each other.

As someone once said, "A smile is rest to the weary, daylight to the discouraged, sunshine to the sad, and an antidote for trouble." A smile is a great, inexpensive gift we can give. Its value, however, is beyond measure. Ask God to show you who needs a smile most today. The next time you see someone without a smile, give them one of yours—real or on a stick. Be prepared—they may be too surprised to even respond, but they will remember it. Besides, a smile is the quickest and least expensive way to improve your appearance!

BE A GO-GO-GO
DANCER

Don't take life seriously;
you won't get out alive!

hen your home is full of clutter and you're feeling drained, put on your favorite upbeat music, turn it up nice and loud, and start moving to the beat as you dance your way through the house. Set a timer and spend only 5 minutes per chore, then go-go-go dancing from room to room. *Go* pick up some clutter. *Go* put something away that's where it shouldn't be. *Go* shake out all the scatter mats you can find.

You might not think so, but in 5 minutes you can accomplish a lot. You can load or unload the dishwasher, clean one shelf in the refrigerator, fold a load of laundry, or organize a junk drawer. You can also set the timer and breeze through your house to see how many items you can discard in 5 minutes. Look for things you don't need or use anymore, items that are broken, and any duplicates you own. What you will discover is getting rid of these things brings an amazing peace. Just last week I received a letter from a mom who had attended my workshop, "How to Organize Your Life and Get Rid of Clutter." She was writing to tell me she had discovered a new joy in giving. She cleared her closet of clothes that don't fit, others she simply doesn't like anymore, and those someone gave her that she hasn't had the heart to get rid of. She even had a big box of maternity clothes she thought were just too nice to give to a regular thrift shop.

She intended to take them to a consignment shop for quite a while (her youngest is four!), but the thought of the hassle and aggravation made her put it off. Then she found out the local Women's Resource Center has a pregnancy division that provides alternatives to abortion and helpful services for expectant moms. Naturally, they were delighted to receive her maternity clothes and the baby clothes she took along. Although she didn't benefit financially, she did experience the delight and joy that comes with giving to someone who really needs it. What a great lesson for her kids, too. As you go-go-go through your home, remember to release what you don't need and share with those who do.

SHAKE YOUR SILLIES OUT!

*Blessed are the flexible for they
will not be bent out of shape.*

AUTHOR UNKNOWN

Our grandkids love to dance and jump about to the Bananas in Pajamas song, "Shake My Sillies Out." When they do, are they flexible! When you've been taking life a bit too seriously, or you feel so rigid you fear you might snap, you may need to wiggle your sillies loose, too. If you're children don't already have this cute song on CD, get it and play it for yourself. Turn it up loud, close the drapes, and boogie to the music. Get over your serious, rational, rigid self and let the sillies take over. If the kids are around, I'm sure you won't have to prompt them to join in with you!

Even if being silly does not come naturally to you, choosing to act silly and having a good laugh at yourself when you're down can give you the fresh perspective you might desperately need. You may not see yourself as a joker or a clown. Maybe you want to have fun but are afraid of what people will think. To overcome these feelings, impersonate someone you know who is happy-go-lucky and carefree. It may be an entertainer, comedian, television personality, relative, or good friend. As you go through your day, ask yourself, "How would that person handle this situation?" or "How would a funny person react?"

Start to see the world the way a humorist or comedian would. They have a knack for turning otherwise upsetting events and embarrassing moments into humorous routines. With a little practice, you can do the same thing. When my little girl, Sheila, was just beginning to talk, she was with me in a crowded department store and happened to notice a nude mannequin, something she had never seen before. After studying it intently, she pointed to the model's chest and hollered at the top of her voice, to the delight of everyone within earshot, "Look, Mommy, you have those!" Although I was embarrassed at first, I kept thinking about what a funny story this would be later.

Learning to have a good laugh at yourself is the first step toward being free to enjoy silliness. Besides, if you haven't had a good laugh at yourself lately, someone else probably has! Loosen up and remember—angels fly because they take themselves lightly.

Imagine how your life would be different if you would devote an entire day to some lighthearted silliness! If a telemarketer calls your house and asks, "How are you today?" say, "I'm glad you asked. It's been a really tough day and I haven't had anyone to talk to. Would you mind listening for a bit?" When the kids come home from school, pick up a banana from the fruit bowl, hold it to your ear and say "Hello? Hello?" Then pass it to one of them and say, "It's for you!" They may roll their eyes and cast you a look that says, "Mom has finally gone over the deep end!" But you're bound to get at least a snicker. Buy a package of smiley-face stickers and put one on the back of every envelope you mail. Use them especially when paying bills that drain your checking account and on the notes you leave for your children!

Start celebrating your half-birthdays. Children and seniors observe them openly. Kids will always tell you they are five and a half or eleven and a half, and our grandparents remind us (and rightly so!) they are ninety-nine and a half. Well, we can do it, too. Exactly six months after your real birthday, buy a cake, go out for dinner, or have a party. Why not start a tradition by doing it for everyone in the family?

For today, do something outlandish, unconventional, and out of character for you. Be absurd. Start developing the habit of thinking wild…weird…wacky…off the wall. Being silly and ridiculous means being child*like* not child*ish*. When the chores, bills, squabbles, teething troubles, and flat tires of life get you down, don't get grumpy—get goofy! Put an orange wedge in your mouth and grin!

RETREAT WITH
THE KIDS

*The best things you can give children,
next to good habits, are good memories.*

SYDNEY J. HARRIS

njoying a retreat doesn't always mean getting away from the kids. My friend Mary, who writes for a large newspaper, told me, "One of my favorite things to do in the evening after a demanding day at the office is to crawl into bed with my daughter for a special time of reading together. We change into our pajamas, grab a beloved bedtime story or children's novel, spend time cuddling, and take turns reading to each other—she reads one page, I read the opposite one. We get goofy with sound effects and character voices until we laugh ourselves silly!" Mary and her daughter both agree that not only are they having a fun and relaxing time together, they are making great memories and, as an added bonus, her daughter's reading skills are noticeably improving.

One evening, have everyone put on housecoats and slippers, and curl up together with a giant bowl of popcorn, or mugs of hot chocolate and marshmallows, to watch a family movie. Your kids, more than likely, have their favorites so let them choose which ones you'll view. They've probably watched them often, but kids look forward to seeing the same movie over and over again, especially with you. They'll get a kick out of being able to tell you what's coming up in the next scene, and it can be fun to hear about it from their perspectives.

Spending unhurried family time can do wonders. In summertime, go out into the backyard, lay on a blanket to study the clouds, and try to identify familiar shapes. Go for a walk and enjoy an ice cream cone or Popsicle together. Swing on a tree swing. Use the slide and teeter totter at a park, or take a dip in the wading pool. Visit the zoo. Go to a local beach with pails and shovels and build sandcastles. Blow bubbles or try to get each other with water-squirt toys. In the evening, study the stars and collect fireflies in jars (be sure to let them go!). In wintertime, if there's snow where you live, take the kids outdoors to make snow angels, build snowmen, go tobogganing, or ice skate on an outdoor rink. When the weather is stormy, stay inside by the fireplace with a cup of hot cocoa to play a game of Scrabble or Monopoly, or to assemble a jigsaw puzzle together. In autumn, visit a fall carnival fair and ride the merry-go-round. Rake up huge piles of autumn leaves for the sole purpose of jumping into them. Go for a country drive to visit a pumpkin farm. Let the children pick out sweet corn and apples at a roadside stand. When spring arrives, put on your rubber boots, grab an umbrella, and go outside during a rain shower to splash in puddles. On a sunny day, go for a bike ride and turn it into a treasure hunt. If the weather is nasty, visit a bowling alley or the library. Stop in at your local hobby shop and check out the train sets, dollhouses, and model-car kits that you may want to try someday. See if a local theater is offering a live children's production. You'll enjoy it just as much as the kids do.

Word puzzles and guessing games are fun anytime, but especially when you're in the car together. Start your own collection of brainteasers, jokes, and riddles. Sing your favorite tunes and record them—just for laughs or send the tape to a far-away relative. Get out the crayons, finger paints, art paper, and craft supplies and let your imagination soar. If you take pictures of your events together, you can assemble a photo album or scrapbook. You'll double your fun when you enjoy your terrific memories later on!

GET DOWN

*The work can wait while you show
your child a butterfly.*

The butterfly won't wait while you work.

hen my toddlers sat on the floor to play with their favorite toys, they invariably called for me to come and sit down with them. Feeling as though I really couldn't afford the time to actually sit and play, I would come close and stoop over them, demonstrating my interest while also letting them know nonverbally that this encounter was temporary. I was, after all, planning to get back to what was really important—my own tasks. To show me "temporary" wasn't good enough, those chubby little toddler hands would firmly pat the floor letting me know unmistakably that I was to *get down*—showing me exactly where I was to sit! Oh, it was so hard to resist, and I am glad to say that most times, I did not.

Something special happens when we meet kids at their level. When we get down with them, we begin to see what we wouldn't see otherwise. Of course, we see the dust bunnies, cracker crumbs, doggie biscuits, and the baby's binky that went missing last Christmas. But more than that, we see what our child sees. Best of all, we see our child!

Take a 5-minute retreat and get down. Sit cross-legged and show genuine interest in whatever your child is engaged in. Stretch out on your tummy on the floor and watch your child do the same. Children love it when you are like them! I can remember trying to do floor exercises along with a TV fitness guru, attempting to lose those last 10 pounds of baby fat, while a toddler was making every effort to stay balanced on my tummy. She thought it was great fun that mommy would get down in her world and wanted to enjoy every minute of the experience.

Roll around on the floor together. Have a good old-fashioned pillow fight or a tickle fest. Giggle like a child. Explore like a child. Reconnect with that part of you that is still a child. When you need a fresh perspective on a problem you are dealing with, entering into the viewpoint of a child may just be what you need.

You can get down outside, too. Dig in the dirt and make mud pies. Take off your shoes and socks and wiggle your toes in the earth. Walk in the wet grass in your bare feet. Make daisy chains. Jump in a rain puddle. Roll down a grassy hill.

While you're at it, include your pets and let them join in the fun. Stroke the cat. Hug the dog and let him lick your face. Pets need to be pampered and played with, too. Their silly antics are bound to be stress-relievers. "Animals are such agreeable friends," said George Eliot. "They ask no questions, they pass no criticisms."

Your children may not remember how tidy the house was, whether the beds got made, or if the laundry was folded, but they will always remember the times you got down on the floor with them.

CELEBRATIONS
AT HOME

Let's have a feast and celebrate.

LUKE 15:23

*I*n our home, we are always on the lookout for a reason to celebrate or get together for a special feast. Birthdays, anniversaries, holidays, graduations, reunions, new homes, new jobs, new babies, new beginnings, good times, and even bad times that have ended, are all good causes in our family.

We have found with just a little thought and effort, any meal can be turned into a gala event. Get your children involved, too, when preparing for your next dinner party. They can help set the table, make a beautiful centerpiece to go with the theme of your meal, and greet visitors at the door. Having them welcome guests and take their coats is a great opportunity for teaching manners and hospitality.

For loads of fun, have kids make some unique, one-of-a-kind place cards. Start with a supply of old or duplicate photographs you have taken of your guests (of course, this is easiest when you are entertaining family since you will be more likely to have photos on hand) and have the children cut out the faces only. Glue them to matching cut-out magazine pictures of bodies that suit the personality or profession of each individual (office worker, grandmother, baby, baseball player, and so on). The funnier the better! Then, glue the entire picture onto a folded cardboard base to be propped at each place setting. Guests will be delighted to find their seats this way, but your children will have more fun than anyone.

To add a touch of festivity to your celebration, choose gift-wrapped presents as your theme, whether or not it is a special occasion. Gift wrap the entire table by using a plain white or brightly colored tablecloth and lengths of wide ribbon criss-crossed over the table in the same way you would tie a present. Use more ribbon to tie soft, silky bows around your place settings and use for napkin rings. Put small wrapped gifts at each dinner guest's plate (the popular dollar stores are handy for seeking out affordable gifts such as notepads, pens, booklets, candles and holders, picture frames). Use foil-wrapped boxes with glimmering bows in a variety of shapes and sizes for a centerpiece and coordinating smaller wrapped boxes as the bases for candleholders. Sprinkle gold and silver confetti over the rest of the table and your instant party is set to go.

Even a mishap can become part of the fun. For our older daughter's sixteenth birthday, I ordered a huge sheet cake to be picked up from the bakery. As I was carrying it to the house from the car, it slid out one end of the box and flipped upside down, onto the sidewalk. Because no one was there to notice, I picked it up, placed it back in the box, got rid of the dirt, smoothed the frosting, and served it anyway. Finally I confessed, and we still laugh about it at every birthday. It has become part of the tradition of our celebrations at home.

MAKE MEALTIME ENTERTAINING

Feasts are made for laughter.

ECCLESIASTES 10:19 NRSV

ou have to eat anyway, so why not turn family mealtime into an event? For starters, have lunch with the kids outside now and again. Spread a blanket on the grass and have a picnic. On a rainy or cold day, put down a cozy quilt on the family room floor and have a picnic indoors.

Another way to celebrate the pleasures of mealtime is to cook together as a family. There are kitchen tasks that children of all ages can perform. Even the youngest child can grease a pan, fold napkins, or help set the table. Older children can wash and tear lettuce for a salad, shape meatballs, peel and chop vegetables, mash potatoes, and place food in serving dishes. This is a good time to teach children cooking is an art—let them get as creative as they can be.

Start a family tradition for one meal each weekend: Tacos on Friday night, animal-shaped pancakes for Saturday breakfast, spaghetti and meatballs for Sunday supper, and so on. Occasionally plan a meal where family members get to make their dish themselves: a personal-size pizza, a hero sandwich, or an ice cream sundae for dessert. Another fun idea is to plan an entire meal that can be eaten without utensils—soup from a cup; chicken fingers coated with bread crumbs, baked in the oven, and served with sweet and sour sauce; vegetable sticks with ranch dressing; bananas dipped in chocolate sauce for dessert. Try serving dessert first for a change!

Once in a while, retreat from the norm and have an elegant dinner with candlelight, flowers, and your best table settings. This is especially fun to do when your meal is a plain one: hot dogs served on a linen tablecloth with matching napkins in fancy rings; tomato soup and grilled cheese sandwiches on your good china; milk served in stemmed goblets. Instead of plopping food containers on the table, try putting them in unique or unusual dishes: sour cream dip in a hollowed-out green pepper or small cabbage; mayonnaise, mustard, and relish in pottery bowls. I have a collection of small dishes resembling a variety of fruits and vegetables that I use for serving condiments: the bunch of grapes for grape jelly, the apple for applesauce, the tomato for ketchup.

Display a menu for your meal of common foods using creative, overly exaggerated, descriptive phrases like the ones you'd see on the menu of a fine restaurant. Instead of announcing, "Burgers for supper," write, "Scrumptious char-grilled sirloin served on hot-from-the-oven buns with succulent, juicy tomatoes, mouth-watering onions, and garden-fresh lettuce!"

An attractive, inviting table, some decorations, and a good imagination can make any meal an event. Choose to dine rather than just eat! Don't forget to welcome God to the table. Invite Him to be present with you, and thank Him for the food He has provided and for the hands that prepared it.

DINING ALFRESCO

*Nature delights in the most
plain and simple diet.*

JOSEPH ADDISON

here's something innocently indulgent, I find, about eating outdoors. I have to wonder, though, if it hasn't become an endangered pleasure, ranking right up there with the evening stroll, breakfast in bed, Sunday afternoon drives, and reading the morning paper. The way I see it, we have to eat anyway, so why not make it a special occasion by taking our food outside? Whether it's a simple ham and cheese on rye on a paper plate at lunchtime, or a fancy supper with linen, silver, crystal stemware, and candles, the dynamics of mealtime is undeniably altered when it's served outside. Whether you eat on an open veranda, a covered porch, or the backyard patio, or whether you are sitting on a blanket at the beach, a bench in a park, or a secluded spot by the lake, mealtime can be a pause in your day and provide countless pleasant memories.

Even breakfast becomes an event when served outside. The menu doesn't have to be fancy—garden-fresh fruit, muffins and nut breads warm from the oven, butter, a variety of jams and jellies, a selection of juices, and a pot of freshly brewed coffee or tea. When you get up early enough to enjoy the sunrise and hear the birds welcoming in the morning, your day is bound to get off to a good start if you include an alfresco breakfast.

Although I can remember many special meals with family and friends in our dining room or around the old kitchen table, the times we've eaten outside seem to bring more vivid memories and feelings of tranquility, relaxation, and simplicity than any others. The time we took the kids, picked up fish and chips, and drove to the lake to sit under an oak tree; or the day we packed up salads, pickles, old cheese and crusty bread, and picnicked in a nearby park, are much more spectacular in my mind than most of our indoor meals. The evening that Cliff and I enjoyed a late-night Italian spaghetti and meatball supper alone on the porch, after the kids were tucked in bed, complete with flickering candlelight and opera music, is something I will never forget. Eating alfresco puts the wonder of nature back into our modern world.

AN ANNUAL
FRIENDSHIP
LUNCHEON

The cheerful heart has a continual feast.

PROVERBS 15:15

t the start of a new year I was invited by a friend to an out-of-town luncheon she was hosting in her new home. It was a small and intimate affair. Her intent was to help some friends reconnect with each other, introduce new ones to the group, and make it an annual event. She served a simple but beautifully planned meal of sparkling cider, homemade cream of broccoli soup, fresh bread from the bakery, and warm cherry pie with French vanilla ice cream.

What she did not plan was the topic of conversation. Very quickly, we found we all were discussing recent major life changes we had undergone. Amazingly, we discovered each one of us had been through some type of life-altering experience. A mother told how she struggled with the concerns of returning to work now that her children are in school all day. One woman shared the joys and trials that accompanied the starting of her own business—an antique shop and country tearoom she had always dreamed of owning. Another had recently lost her husband after a lengthy illness and, at times, felt the loneliness to be unbearable. A new mom shared the challenges involved in maintaining life-balance, and the guilt of being away from her new baby to attend this luncheon. The hostess told of the extra workload of having a frail and bedridden mother-in-law come to live in her home.

During the course of our meal, no topic was left untouched. Everything from body image, recipes, and diets, to sexuality, relationships, men, in-laws, fitness, vacations, prayer, and faith in God was covered. We shared tears and laughter and hugs as the afternoon flew by. When it was time to leave, we knew we wanted to be part of this experience again next year.

For days afterward, I relished the allure of that luncheon. It seems the biggest discovery of the day was that we are not alone, as varied as our lifestyles are, we have so much in common. Sometimes, it's possible to get into our own little corner of the world and start imagining that everyone else has somehow achieved the ideal life we have only dreamed of. We're the ones left on the outside, still striving and longing to have what we believe others have supposedly attained. Then when we come together as a group, we see there really is no truth to it. There is no perfect or ideal life. Each of us has something to deal with whether it is coming to terms with middle age, encouraging insecure teens, being there for adult children, concerns over a grandchild being bullied, or struggling with a marital dilemma. Strangely, knowing we are not alone somehow helps ease the burden. Only now do I realize how much we had been yearning for this type of fellowship.

Plan to connect with friends sometime soon. Heaven knows, we need each other.

THE FRIENDSHIP TEA

*Over cups of tea, I listened to my friend
and my friend heard me. My joy was
hers and hers was mine, as we shared
our hearts line by line.*

AUTHOR UNKNOWN

hile I put the kettle on," my friend Margaret would say to me, "why don't you tell me all about it?" I can picture the scene in my mind's eye as if it were only yesterday, although in reality it was several years ago. With open arms and a generous heart, she'd invite me to relax at her comfortable kitchen table. Over steamy mugs of tea, she'd listen compassionately as I vented my concerns about being a single mom, the longing I had in my heart to provide my two little girls with a good home and positive upbringing, and the uncertainty I felt about our finances and our future. Along with the tea, there was almost certainly a basket filled with freshly baked tea buns still warm from the oven, served with my friend's own homemade strawberry jam or grape jelly. Aside from the conversation, there was invariably a good deal of prayer, plenty of hugs, a Scripture passage or two, and shared tears of both laughter and sorrow. Somehow, I always came away with renewed hope, a stronger faith, and a clearer understanding of God's love for me. As I look back, it seems those conversations were very one-sided, but Margaret never let on or seemed to mind. As our friendship grew and evolved, it became more of a two-way street. I was privileged to make tea for her as she shared with me some of her own concerns and challenges.

Today, years later, whenever I steep a pot of tea for someone in need of encouragement, I vividly recall those precious moments of love and understanding at Margaret's kitchen table. "Friends," said Charlotte Gray, "put the whole world right over a cup of tea."

During my growing-up years, when problems needed to be solved in our home, you could always hear the phrase "Let's make a pot of tea." My mother believed having a cup of tea together was the solution to just about any predicament or dilemma. Anytime Mom was in the kitchen with a friend, and we heard the teakettle whistling, we knew better than to interrupt. It was the signal that a heart-to-heart talk was about to take place and lives would most likely be changed forever.

Is there someone you know who would benefit by sharing a pot of tea? There's no need to fuss. Pastries can come from your favorite bakery, and jams and jellies from a local market. It's the mere ceremony of teatime that provides the opportunity to mull over the true nature of things, inviting us to think about what is really important, and bringing us closer in touch with each other. Sipping tea restores balance and harmony in our lives, and our situation takes on a fresh perspective. We return to our families and our circumstances with renewed faith and optimism. Why not invite someone for an intimate friendship tea today? As my mom would say, "Have a cup of tea, and you'll feel better."

GROWN-UP TEA PARTIES

Tea is the drink of friendship.

SARAH JANE EVANS

hen we were growing up, my sister and I enjoyed a backyard tea party every chance we got. We would get decked out in our finest attire, bejeweled with trinkets from the dress-up trunk, including floppy-brimmed hats, threadbare evening bags, and oversized high-heeled shoes. Out would come the miniature china tea set, a pretty embroidered, lace-trimmed tablecloth, and the teddy bear and rag doll "guests" that were seated on either side of us around our child-sized table. Of course, "tea" was actually apple, orange, or pineapple juice. Our mother would supply us with tiny peanut butter and banana pinwheel sandwiches, celery and carrot sticks, and a few chewy oatmeal cookies. A deep friendship was born between my sister and me during those tea parties, and I am forever grateful for the role they played in our relationship.

Today, over steamy cups of tea, the friendship my sister and I share keeps on growing, producing a soothing wellspring of support and comfort for us both. In this harried, nerve-racking world, we can be thankful for one of the small rituals of intimacy that still exists—the grown-up tea party. As adults, when we join friends to sip cups of tea—in front of a blazing fire protected from a blustery winter's day, or on the back porch on a lazy summer afternoon—

these quiet moments of communion tie our hearts together. The genuine caring and gentle acceptance we offer each other over cups of tea represent in us the very heart of God.

Take time for tea—now. We can't wait for our lives to slow down, for all the emergencies to end, for circumstances to be ideal before we do it. How often do we greet each other at the mall or in line at the bank and say, "When things settle down, we'll have to get together," or, "When life gets back to normal, let's have tea." Once the baby is sleeping through the night, done with teething, finished getting her shots, gets toilet trained…then it should work. When the kids are back in school, the laundry is caught up, I get the house organized, maybe then I'll find some time. Let's face it. We can't wait for the timing to be perfect, for things to become normal again. This *is* normal for most of us!

Maybe you can't regulate all the craziness in your life. Maybe some of it is truly beyond your control. But you don't have to be a passive victim, pushed about by the world's frantic pace. Remind yourself that by taking time for friends, for peace, for quiet moments, for something as simple as a cup of tea, you'll be restoring the balance in your life that is missing. Whether you plan to have tea to celebrate someone's birthday, the arrival of a new season, a special holiday, or just for the love of friendships, do it soon—do it often. After all, "the mere clink of cups and saucers," George Gissing tells us, "turns the mind to happy repose." And repose is truly what we're after.

PART 8

REFLECTIONS OF COMFORT

BE HERE NOW

*The thought of some work runs in my head and I
am not where my body is—I am
out of my senses.*

HENRY DAVID THOREAU

ow often are we somewhere in body but somewhere else in our thoughts? Without even knowing it, we can be "out of our senses." I remember a particular time when my children were small and I had decided to devote a couple of weeks to doing some heavy spring-cleaning and serious organizing in our home. After a few days, I realized how little time I had been spending with the family and decided to drop everything to go for a fun picnic in the park. Later, with the blanket spread and the picnic lunch laid out, I found myself thinking, "What am I doing here with all that work at home waiting to be done?" I was "out of my senses."

So often, we are not in spirit where we are in our bodies. In our thoughts, we are somewhere we believe we *should* be rather than where we are presently. When we're working, we long to be spending time with our families. When we do take time out, we can't seem to let go of the nagging thoughts of chores that need to be done and the to-do lists that never end. When you do that to yourself, you never get to enjoy either place. To get the most from the moment, practice being where you are.

Ever so gradually I have been training myself to bring my awareness back to the activity I am presently involved in. By doing so, moment-by-moment and step-by-step, I am finding a peace I never knew existed. I remember the day my young daughter helped me learn this lesson. When Lori was about five years old, she came into the kitchen to share with me something she was concerned about. It was supper time and I was peeling potatoes. My mind in a dozen different places: the piles of laundry that needed to be washed before morning, lunches that had to be packed for the next day, the project I would be working on after dinner. As Lori chattered away by my feet, I attempted to make all the appropriate noises and "uh-huh's" to let her know I was listening. She, being more perceptive than I anticipated, turned around to leave, saying, "Never mind, Mommy. I'll tell you later when you can really listen." Needless to say, I quickly dropped the potatoes, brought her back with a big hug, and took 5 minutes to *really* listen.

When we don't listen, not only do we cheat ourselves of the moment, but others who depend on us can sense that we are miles away in our thoughts. Being there in spirit can be a 5-minute retreat that allows us to connect—with those we cherish, those who love us, and those who count on us. True beauty in life is found when we remember yesterday, dream of tomorrow, but live for today!

A FEW OF YOUR
FAVORITE THINGS

My coat and I live comfortably together.
It has assumed all my wrinkles, does not hurt
me anywhere, has molded itself to my
deformities, is complacent to all
my movements, and I only feel its presence
because it keeps me warm. Old coats and old
friends are the same thing.

VICTOR HUGO

egardless of our personal decorating styles, our homes should be shelters we can retreat to any time of day, where we can enjoy our favorite things and escape the tensions of the world. Sadly, with our hectic family schedules, including a sink full of dirty dishes that didn't make it into the dishwasher, wall-to-wall toys, sticky floors, cookie crumbs on the sofa, and beds that rarely get made, our homes can often become the very place we want to avoid.

Think about your personal refuge. Is your home a place where you love to spend time because it's inviting, cozy and filled with all the comforts that make you feel snug and secure? If not, consider what appeals to you, what you long for, and ways you can create your own safe haven to soothe both body and soul.

At long last, I now have a workspace in my home that has become my refuge. The desk where I spend much of my time writing has a fireplace on one side and a window on the other side, which overlooks our wooded backyard. Across the room is a baby grand piano, inherited from my grandmother, which I play for a few moments here and there whenever I need a mini-break. Within reach are my much-loved books and a collection of favorite magazines, so there is always something interesting or enlightening to read. In plain view, are the plants and artwork I find calming and inspiring. Today, a china teapot and steamy cup of earl grey tea are nearby, and from the corner of my eye, I can see the flickering of a candle on my tea tray. I've discovered what a blessing it is to be surrounded by a few of my favorite things.

With a little thought and imagination, you can turn your home into a haven of comfort. Make it so cozy you won't want to leave whenever you have the choice! Create a list of the comforts you enjoy. Is it plenty of bookcases and places to display your favorite things? You may want to have some plump pillows, an afghan or quilt, and a snug place to curl up to encourage you to take a peaceful snooze while the children are napping. Is there a big, comfy chair with a footstool and good lighting that beckons you to sit and read when the timing is just right? Could you use some plants or fresh flowers to cheer up an otherwise dreary corner? Think about homes you may have visited in the past that made you feel welcome and figure out what appealed to you. Chances are comfort was a common denominator. Make a list of your favorite things and begin creating your personal haven. You'll enjoy your 5-minute retreats even more!

REMINDERS OF GOD'S GOODNESS

*And you must commit yourselves wholeheartedly
to these commands I am giving you today.
Repeat them again and again to your
children....Write them on the doorposts of
your house and on your gates.*

DEUTERONOMY 6:6,9 NLT

ith a little effort, we can create an atmosphere in our homes that helps our families to be reminded of God's blessings and to focus on the positive side of life. When my two girls and I first lived on our own after my devastating marriage breakdown, one thing that helped keep us strong was to be surrounded by Scripture verses and inspiring quotes. I wrote them on recipe cards and posted them around the house—inside kitchen cabinets, on the bathroom mirror, over the sink. At a glance, I could read aloud a word of encouragement, and we would all be strengthened by God's goodness and faithfulness. These reminders helped get us through many struggles with loneliness, heartache, and uncertainty, and restored joy and hope in our home.

Even today, when I receive a pretty greeting card from a friend or family member, I place it where I can see it as a daily reminder that I am loved and thought about. Sometimes I make it a point to memorize the words on the card, and often I have the opportunity to pass these words of support on to someone who would benefit. I strategically place some of my favorite books around my home, where I can see their motivating or inspirational titles. An open Bible with verses underlined or highlighted can be found in most rooms. Each time I enter a room, there is at least one object in plain view acting as a reminder to stay focused on possibilities and positive expectations.

Toys from childhood can also help revive pleasant memories of bygone days. If you have some, get them from the box in the attic and use them to decorate the rooms of your home. Share the stories of each one with your children—who gave it to you, when you got it, what it meant to you as a child. A friend has a wicker doll carriage in her living room filled with stuffed teddy bears she snuggled with as a youngster. My husband has his antique train set on display, and we have a spare bedroom decorated just for our grandchildren with toys from our past. It's comforting to reminisce about the fun we had playing as children.

We all need to be reminded to stay positive when life starts getting us down. One very talented friend enjoys stenciling as a hobby and has the fruits of the Spirit from the book of Galatians—love, joy, peace, patience, kindness, goodness, faithfulness, gentleness, and self-control—stenciled around the top of her dining room walls, adorned with garlands of flowers and vines. There are several wallpaper borders available that have this same Bible scripture plus other inspiring verses on them.

Why not start placing positive reminders throughout your home to encourage yourself and the whole family?

REFLECTIONS OF
THE REAL YOU

*The soaps in the bathroom, the flowers in the
garden, the book on the bedside table are all
strong symbols of a life in progress.*

CHARLOTTE MOSS

The possessions in your home express the true you, from the fabrics, colors, and patterns in your decorating choices, to the furnishings and accessories in each room, plants in your garden, dishes in your cabinet, knickknacks on your windowsill, pictures on your walls, and books on your shelves. It's been said that you can tell a lot about a person by her library—the novels, magazines, and newspapers sitting around. But do those and other details in your home really reflect who you are, or are you still bound by choices you made years ago? Have you outgrown some of the things that furnish and adorn your house? Maybe you are still living with pieces from your childhood home or gifts that don't really suit you but you feel obligated to keep and display. Perhaps you've become so accustomed to your belongings that you don't really know whether or not they represent your true nature. It may not be something you've put a lot of thought into, yet surroundings do affect the way you feel about your life, the way you respond to your family, and whether or not you are content and at ease in your home.

I remember visiting one family that moved every year for career reasons. Because money was not a consideration, they were able to sell everything in their home and start fresh with each new place. Although I'm not sure I would want to live that way on a continual basis, I was intrigued by the thought of what it would be like to furnish and decorate a home from scratch—I had never been in that position. It got me thinking about the choices I would make if I were ever able to do so. Would I want to keep some favorites from my existing home or start completely new in every room? Would any of the pieces I now own fit my new décor or would I want to go with a totally different style? Am I tolerating some things simply because they were gifts, or passed down from other generations? By asking these questions, my personal preferences started to emerge for the first time.

For 5 minutes today, mentally take inventory of your possessions. Envision yourself in a home that is completely empty, going from room to room filling closets, cupboards, cabinets, and drawers with only those things you would enjoy. Which linens, glassware, cutlery, and china patterns would you want to use? What type of wardrobe would you choose? Which artwork, candles, furniture fabrics, colors, and patterns make you feel calm and restful? Use your imagination and let your creativity go wild. Determine which accessories depict the real you, portraying your personal style and the atmosphere you are aiming to project in your home. Maybe it's time to start cleaning out the old to make room for the new. Gradually clear out what doesn't make you feel at peace and lovingly donate items to an organization that will distribute them to needy families. Choose to keep and purchase only those strong symbols that truly represent who you really are—a life in progress.

TAKE TIME
TO DREAM

*The gift of fantasy has meant more to
me than my talent for absorbing
absolute knowledge.*

ALBERT EINSTEIN

f you were called a daydreamer as a child, it probably wasn't a compliment! Even today, it seems we are embarrassed if we are caught in a moment of repose. We are mortified to think that someone might interpret it as "goofing off." There's a mania that has swept our world to be productive and effective at all times, to make use of every spare minute. Being crazy busy has become a status symbol—we almost wear it as a badge of honor.

One mom squeezes in computer lessons on the only morning she isn't working. Another wedges volunteer jobs into an already impossible agenda. We cram our kids' schedules with sports, music lessons, after-school clubs, and swimming classes. Even they have started carting around little Disney character day planners and organizers complete with to-do lists. Planners can be helpful tools when it comes to motivating our kids to plan ahead, stay on target, avoid missed deadlines, and keep track of their papers and other belongings. And after-school activities are important. But if it is at the expense of a little down time, when imagination has a chance to soar and creativity turns into innovative problem solving, is it really such a good idea to have each day scheduled down to the minute?

Writers, composers, artists, designers, and research scientists, whose jobs are to dream into existence what isn't already there, know the value of daydreaming. When I reach a block in my writing, I could chain myself to my computer in an attempt to force ideas, but all that would emerge is gibberish. On the other hand, I have discovered if I let it all go, take a break, and simply daydream, ideas come rushing in like a flood. Miraculously, tangled thoughts unravel themselves in my head while I stand in the shower, go for a drive, take a walk, pray and meditate, or simply sit and stare out a window.

We all need creative thought for even the most routine, commonplace problems. I could rack my brain trying to figure out how to alleviate my daughter's insecurities at school, set up a better file system for household papers, settle a spat with my mother-in-law, or keep the kids from causing a racket while I am on the telephone. But it's only when I am strolling by the lake watching a glorious sunset, that God has a chance to get my attention. Answers come floating to me, clear and simple.

When was the last time you drifted off for 5 minutes into your own private world, when you didn't feel under pressure to explain yourself? Let down your defenses. Give your mind the freedom to meander. I'm not suggesting we ignore our responsibilities, lose our focus, and lounge all day in our pajamas. We need to find a balance between our "up time" and our "down time." When we keep working without a break, our minds are inhibited by common sense and logic. Not all problems succumb to customary solutions. As we frantically attempt to organize ourselves, we ought to leave enough time for doing nothing but daydreaming. And we should encourage others, especially our children, to do the same.

CHOOSE
CONTENTMENT

egrettably, many of us have not learned "in whatever state we are, to be content." We are convinced that something else has to take place in order for us to be satisfied. First, we believe we'll be happy once we get married and have babies. Then, we'll be happier when those babies sleep through the night, survive teething, grow out of diapers, know how to dress themselves, put their toys away, go to school, leave home…get married! We tell ourselves that life will be better once we're out of debt, when our husbands treat us better, when we buy bigger houses, drive nicer cars, and get to have that dream vacation at last. Finally, we're sure we'll experience true happiness when the mortgage is paid off and we retire. How sad it is when we put our happiness on hold until we get to the final years of our lives. It's as if we hope to hear a booming voice from the heavens saying, "Your life is now perfect. You may go ahead and start to live!"

The truth is there will always be challenges to face. In fact, right now in your own home, you are either in the middle of handling a problem, you have just left a problem, or you are headed toward the next problem. These are the only three places you can be! So, if you are not dealing with some sort of predicament this minute, don't panic. It's on the way—guaranteed! Enjoy the 5-minute interim.

When we lack contentment, it's most often caused by one of two things: continually striving to reach a problem-free state or desiring to own more than what we have. Henry David Thoreau said, "I make myself rich by making my wants few." I remember a time when this became especially clear to me. After completing a particularly frenzied period of exciting growth in my speaking career, I visited our shopping center for the first time in a few years. I had been traveling full-time speaking at international events, so my husband and daughters had helped out by picking up the things on my shopping list. Other than that, I ordered from catalogs or purchased what I needed while on tour. What I experienced when I finally went to the mall could only be called *culture shock*. I was stunned by what I saw. The countless choices in each store left me staggering. The shocking number of items available made it difficult to make decisions. Even worse than that, I began to focus on all that I *didn't* have. Suddenly, I wondered if I needed a new "this" or a better "that." I went home feeling deprived, as though the rest of the world must be enjoying all the latest in luxuries while I did without! I hadn't felt my "lack" until that day in the mall.

What is causing your unhappiness? Is it a feeling of being short-changed, or that you are missing out on some of the finer things life has to offer? How can you turn the tide of discontent? Start by making a conscious effort to savor the ordinary treasures that come your way—a baby's giggle, a toddler's chubby cheek pressed against yours, the smell of pot roast in the oven, a frolicking puppy, a coffee break on the back porch—alone! Capture the joy of the moment. For example, you found a few moments to sit and read this book. Relish the experience rather than focusing on what you'd rather have in the future. Resist the urge to complain. It's too easy to fall into the "victim" trap, seeing yourself as unfortunate, poor, hard-done-by, or powerless. Instead, cherish the good things you have now in your life. Acknowledge your achievements and celebrate them. Reward yourself. Even the smallest accomplishment deserves recognition, whether you called your sister, cleaned out the fish tank, paid off a loan, spent time playing a game of Scrabble with your child, cleaned the kitchen, completed a work project ahead of a deadline, or got the oil changed in the car.

Appreciating what you have and where you are does not require a Pollyanna mentality. It's not about pie-in-the-sky thinking or seeing life through rose-colored glasses. It is about learning, in whatever state you are, to be content!

AN ATTITUDE
OF GRATITUDE

"It's snowing still," said Eeyore gloomily.
"And freezing. However," he said, brightening
up a little, "we haven't had an earthquake lately."

EEYORE, THE HOUSE AT POOH CORNER

ne evening as I stood at the kitchen counter preparing dinner, I began to think about how a spirit of thankfulness could change the way I approach everyday tasks and even the way I treat the people dearest to me. Instead of falling into my usual grumbling—"I spend more time cooking and cleaning up than we spend at the dinner table"—I consciously tried to alter my viewpoint. "How blessed I am to have a wonderful family to cook for, nutritious food to put on the table, and a warm, cozy kitchen to eat in." It took just as long to cook the meal, and dinner was over as quickly as always, but I felt a new level of contentment. Throughout the next day, I was amazed by how often I could apply the spirit of thankfulness and express gratitude, instead of exasperation. When handling the mundane aspects of my day like folding laundry and making a bed, I found myself expressing thankfulness for the member of the family connected to each item. My auto-pilot responses to the frustrations of missed school buses and undone homework were replaced with more caring, compassionate, problem-solving approaches.

Gratitude and inner peace seem to go hand in hand. Counting our blessings generates a feeling of abundance. Thinking grateful thoughts reminds us that our lives are already filled with so much of what we want and need. Without gratitude, we fall into the trap of focusing on scarcity, lack, and hardship, which leads to complaints and more problems.

Keeping a thanksgiving journal is one way to stay focused on blessings. Make a list of the things you are grateful for at the end of each day. Acknowledge and appreciate whatever you currently have that brings you pleasure, peace, joy, and contentment, as well as situations that help you to grow. Write out a daily blessing list and post it on the refrigerator. Refer to your list whenever you are feeling down as a reminder that, even if everything is not going smoothly, your life really is overflowing with good things. It's not difficult to create a full inventory of what you are thankful for. I am grateful for my health, husband, children, career, my audiences and readers, freedom, and a heavenly Father who loves me. You might be thankful for a child's laugh, an invitation to dinner, a pet that gives you unconditional love. Maybe it's finding out that the washing machine can be repaired after all, the lab test came back negative, the toilet didn't overflow, the baby finally stopped crying, the check didn't bounce, the lost dog found his way home, and the only reason you had a call from the school was see if you would chaperone the bus trip to the zoo.

Think of people you are grateful for—the lady who let you in line at the grocery store when she noticed your toddler was in need of her nap, the driver who allowed you to merge into traffic, the auto mechanic who said he'd fix it for free this time. When I opened my mail yesterday, there was a note from a friend telling me that my recipe for butternut squash soup was a big hit at her family dinner. Now she's got me thinking. There's a lady I've wanted to thank for a long time. In the lakeside town where I take my morning walk, I pass by her extraordinary yard situated in an otherwise ordinary neighborhood. Her amazing array of beautiful flowers, shrubs, bushes, and other plants behind a white picket fence always uplifts me and makes me smile. I think I'll take note of her address next time I go by and drop her a line.

Take a minute to write a simple note of thanks when you've been a guest in someone's home, or better yet, surprise someone with a thank-you note when they've been to your house. Write it out shortly after they leave, letting them know how much you enjoyed having them in your home and how much you appreciate their friendship. Send thank-you notes for intangible things, too. "I'm grateful for our friendship," "Thank you for being there when I needed a hug," or "Thanks for being such a great kid!"

Get the whole family involved. Let them hear you use the words *thankful* or *grateful* often. Tell someone you are thankful to be home or you're grateful to be able to spend the evening together. If your child is grouchy, have him tell you something he can be thankful for. Spend time around the dinner table sharing with each other the things you are grateful for that happened during the day. Gratitude is contagious. When one child expresses that he's grateful his mittens kept his hands warm while playing in the snow, another remembers she found the library book that was missing for three days.

The more gratitude you express, the more you have to be grateful for. Life has a way of presenting us with greater benefits when we're thankful for the smallest ones. Thank God for the beauty all around you and for the gift of life. When you begin and end each day with words of thanksgiving on your lips, it's nearly impossible to feel anything but harmony and inner peace. Prayer warrior Julie Billiart expressed it well when she said, "How the good God loves those who appreciate the value of His gifts."

CAPTURE YOUR THOUGHTS IN WRITING

*My journal is that of me which would
else spill over and run to waste.*

HENRY DAVID THOREAU

The concept of journaling was introduced to me 20 years ago when I began attending seminars and workshops similar to the ones I now present. I found not only did I want to record the ideas and principles introduced by the presenter, but I also wanted to capture thoughts that came to me while I listened. It was as though something deep inside me was stirred and challenged by sitting in an atmosphere of motivation and inspiration. I wanted to get those impressions in writing while they were fresh. Eventually I developed the habit of carrying a small, spiral-bound notebook with me at all times. Whenever I hear a keynote address at a conference, an after-dinner message at a banquet, or a sermon on Sunday morning, I can record the speaker's thoughts as well as my own. I am convinced that these are times when God whispers insights and heavenly wisdom to my heart. As I refer to my notes later on, I often get new direction in life choices, guidance in decision-making, and solutions to problems when it appeared there were none. The entries are dated and remind me of what was important at that time. They are also a way to measure my progress in various areas of personal, professional, and spiritual growth.

Now I write most every day. I record impressions of my day, words of wisdom I've come across, experiences, observations, and reflections. When God gives me insights as I read the Bible and other spiritual literature, as I meditate, or in daily experiences, I jot those down. I am not a slave to my journal nor do I get too upset if I miss a day or even a week. Some days I simply prefer to sit quietly and read past entries. They remind me of all I have to be thankful for—the miracles, the answered prayers, and the goodness that surrounds me. When I pick up a pen and open my journal, my heart opens as well. Journaling is a practical way to learn and listen to God's voice.

Slowing down during your day to journal allows your body to rest, focuses your mind, and gives your spirit a chance to function in its original role. Being able to put your experiences into words is good for your physical health, too. It seems that we recover more quickly after traumatic events—a teenager's car accident or the loss of a pet—when we put our feelings down on paper.

Start by jotting down whatever comes to your mind that helps you withdraw from the world. Here's a habit I borrowed from my husband. He makes a conscious effort each day to find one unique moment to relish, whether it's the chubby chipmunk that's come out to eat the peanuts he placed on the front walk or the crunch of his favorite brand of apple as he takes that first bite. After watching him, I now do it for myself. I record these images, feelings, and thoughts in my journal. Write about your emotions, happy or sad. Seeing them in print can often help you sort them out. Once you put your hopes and fears on paper, you have something tangible to deal with rather than having mere thoughts and feelings floating around inside you. It's a positive way to deal with negative emotions without turning them inward, bottling them up, or lashing out at loved ones.

Chronicle the details of your day—from the mundane to the miraculous, from the washer and dryer that both broke down on the same day to baby's first step. Record the peaks and the valleys. Describe your dreams, goals, and plans. Keeping a journal means you always have a safe place to be alone with your thoughts. On the other hand, it may become the story of your life, handed down to your children and theirs. Don't obsess about privacy. You can lock it away in a drawer or some other secret place, or write with others in mind and choose to leave it as a legacy.

As you create your journal, aside from the narratives, include wise quotes, humorous sayings, key phrases, one-liners, cute things the kids said or did, out of the ordinary things to do on weekends, or fun places to go for summer vacation. Add pictures, drawings, sketches, and photographs. The beauty of journaling is its flexibility. Start small and add to it daily or weekly. Most importantly, write when you are moved and inspired.

You may want to consider investing in a special book with an attractive cover. If it looks enticing, you might be more motivated to make entries often. Instead of an old plastic pen with the end chewed, treat yourself to the most beautiful pen your budget will allow. (You may want to weld it to your journal!) Whether you choose a formal, hard-covered book from a stationery store, a spiral bound notepad, or a 3-ring binder filled with paper, the act of journaling can be a life-altering experience. Return to your creation every day or as often as you can. Then just sit. Listen thoughtfully. Wait in a state of confident expectation. Soon you will have a personal chronicle of delight and joy, laughter and tears...a record of your amazing life.

CREATE A
JOY LIST

They shall obtain joy and gladness,
and sorrow and sighing shall flee away.

Isaiah 35:10 rsv

The important thing to remember about joy is if you don't have it, you can't share it. If you are unhappy, you can't give happiness. If you are dissatisfied, you can't offer contentment. When you are filled with regrets, you can't offer hope. Nor can you receive those things. Let's face it, when you're feeling down and out, that's what you project to the world. And what you give, amazingly, returns to you, often multiplied. This can be good or bad news. One of God's laws says that whatever you sow, you will also reap. Think about what seeds you have been planting and how you can begin sowing from a full heart rather than an empty one.

The next time you are trying to give even though your gauge reads empty, create an inventory of blissful delights that would fill you up again, bringing you peace, joy, and contentment. Plan to allow yourself some privacy each day, even if it's only 5 minutes at a time, indulging in at least one innocent pleasure. Get yourself a pretty journal and a good pen, sit comfortably somewhere, and write out your joy list. It might look something like this:

- Take a long walk

- Buy a bouquet of flowers

- Wear pretty lingerie

- Call a friend

- Watch a goofy TV show or funny movie

- Play music, turn it up loud, and dance like crazy

- Snuggle up in bed with a good book

- Sink into a tub for a long luxurious soak at the end of the day

- Go for a bike ride in a quiet neighborhood

- Have a facial and mini-makeover at the mall

- Go on a shopping spree for additions to your wardrobe

- Get a new hairdo, manicure, or pedicure

- Run on the beach

- Sleep late

- Have an afternoon nap

When your life seems mired in piles of washing and dirty dishes, when you are yearning to spend time with people who won't throw temper tantrums or demand your constant attention, go to your list. Pick one thing. In your journal write an affirmation to yourself: "I, (fill in your name), now enjoy one nurturing 5-minute retreat." Pamper yourself. Be true to yourself, and you'll have more to give when you return.

THE ART OF PUTTERING
AND PONDERING

To putter is to discover.

ALEXANDRA STODDARD

hen I get lost in puttering and pondering on a Saturday morning, it's as though I have entered some other dimension—a serene, unperturbed, and hassle-free one. In a world of my own, with a freshly brewed pot of coffee nearby, I am oblivious to the passing of time. The cares of the previous week seem to dissipate. At one time, I felt guilty for devoting so much attention and effort to such an unproductive activity as puttering—a seemingly senseless undertaking that would never even warrant showing up on my to-do list. I now see puttering as a blessing. While it may appear that I am only sorting, sifting, and spending a few moments getting my house in order, my spirit knows better. Puttering provides the breathing space I need to soothe my frantic soul and stressed-out spirit after a week of unending daily activities, hectic schedules, and weighty obligations.

My journey to another time and place often begins as a treasure hunt. I'm still in my bathrobe with coffee cup in hand, and searching through drawers and cupboards for some misplaced item—a recipe I'd like to make tonight, a household tip clipped from a woman's magazine, a coupon tucked away offering a discount on carpet cleaning. Then, in the middle of my search, the mysterious transpires. I get sidetracked and am curiously transported to the "other" side. What sends me off is something different each time. It could be the envelope of photos from someone's birthday celebration or last winter's vacation that somehow didn't make it into the family album (or at least to the holding box where they go for safekeeping, hoping to make it to the album). As I browse through them, I find myself laughing and reliving those treasured moments as though I was right in the middle of them. Or, it might be the stack of letters from the past sent from my sisters and mother, who live at a distance and now send mostly E-mail messages. I continue sifting and sorting through the thank-you notes, cards of encouragement sent from special friends, and love notes Cliff left on the kitchen counter to welcome me home from some business trip (I knew I'd appreciate reading them one more time!). There's children's artwork that once hung on the refrigerator, the gift certificate for a one-hour pedicure I thought I had used, and the advertisement for a play at a local church that I really want to see. My goal becomes to toss out some of this stuff, but I can't bear to part with most of it, so instead I put it back in the drawer. At least this time it's in some semblance of order.

My puttering is going well, and I'm having too much fun to quit now, so I continue. After I poke through some old cookbooks with their treasured recipes, the old standbys all stained and splattered, I jot a quick shopping list of ingredients for this recipe or that one and move on to other rooms. I clean a few brass pieces and rearrange some furniture. Uh-oh. A book catches my eye, one I started ages ago but never finished, and…I'm lost in oblivion once again.

When we were kids, my sister and I came home from school on Fridays to be greeted by the familiar scents of furniture polish and floor wax. It was cleaning day at our house, so we knew we'd find Mom in the midst of her chores. Sure enough, when we rounded the corner into the living room, all the books had been removed from the bookcase, the vacuum cleaner sat in the middle of the room, the dust rag was draped over a chair. And there was Mom—sitting in the midst of it all munching an apple and deeply engrossed in one of the books. Mom knew the value of puttering and pondering. Puttering around the house is really a time to be alone, to daydream, to contemplate, to mull things over, and to get in touch with yourself again. "Ah!" said Jane Austen, "There's nothing like staying home for real comfort."

A TRIP DOWN
MEMORY LANE

*We do not remember days, we remember
moments. The richness of life lies in memories we
have forgotten.*

CESARE PAVESE

eminiscing isn't something we take the time to do. It's usually more than enough for us moms to simply keep up with life's daily demands as we work to build new memories for our families and ourselves. Besides, isn't reminiscing something we save for our old age? We certainly don't have time for such things today. Yet, we can learn so much by reflecting on and embracing our past. Sometimes we become so busy being grown-up that we almost forget that we were once children. But if we were honest with ourselves, we'd have to admit buried beneath our layers of adulthood and experience, lives the same little child from years ago. By acknowledging and celebrating that child within us, we become better equipped to face our lives ahead. Take time to remember a luscious slice of your childhood. Perhaps it was the first time you climbed to the top of the apple tree or that sunny day at the beach when you built the perfect sandcastle. Allow yourself to delight in the memory of simple childhood pleasures. Now take this joy back into adulthood with you.

Spend a few moments traveling back in time with your children. Go on a trip down memory lane. Take them to visit your childhood neighborhood and walk by the house where you lived or the school you attended. Was there a park where you loved to go and swing or use the teeter-totter? Or a convenience store you frequented to buy penny candy and ice cream? Drive past your grandparent's old homestead, follow the bicycle route you took to get to the public swimming pool in summertime, and find the hill you used for sledding on snowy days. Tell your kids stories of when you were young. Describe your relationships with your parents, siblings, aunts, uncles, and cousins. Host a family reunion in your backyard so that the children can get to know the people they hear you talk about.

Reflect on a day when you felt special. We tend to forget that there was ever a day when our life was any different than it is today. However, we've all had accomplishments worth celebrating. Unfortunately, we quickly forget them and move on, sometimes even neglecting to celebrate them at all. Take a moment to remember a time when you felt truly special and share it with your child. Perhaps it was a sporting or academic achievement, a personal victory, or even your wedding day. One mom I know had never thought to show her 10-year-old daughter the photo album she assembled while performing in off-Broadway musical productions before she was married. She got it out while we were visiting in their home one evening, and we all enjoyed browsing through a bit of her past. Best of all, it was a joy to see how delighted her little girl was to be viewing a part of her mom's life she hadn't known much about until then. Allow yourself to relive those cherished moments, and to celebrate them all over again—this time with your children.

Sometimes we feel as if we haven't really accomplished a lot. Yet if we examine our hearts and our photos, and occasionally travel down memory lane, we will have to admit that there have been times when we have enjoyed personal successes worth celebrating with our children!

PRAYER RETREATS

Pray continually.

1 Thessalonians 5:17

have so much to do," said Martin Luther, "that I cannot possibly get by on less than three hours of prayer a day." Mother Teresa said that if her nuns did not pray for several hours every day, they would not have the strength to do their work. Although I can't say that I spend three consecutive hours in prayer each day, I have found the more full my schedule gets, the more time I must devote to prayer.

The Bible says we are to pray without ceasing. Is it really possible to do anything without stopping? In the same way we breathe, swallow, and blink continuously without even thinking about it, I believe we can pray continually as well. Certainly there are those sacred times spent on our knees, pouring out our hearts to the Father and having Him commune with us. But, I have found I pray more with my eyes open—driving in my car, preparing dinner, putting in a load of laundry, unloading the dishwasher, baking muffins, taking a shower. Yes—it is possible to pray without ceasing.

Life is full of challenges, burdens, and suffering way beyond our comprehension, but we can turn to God in every situation, on every occasion. We can take refuge in His loving arms and know that He inspires us to make right decisions. "It is as natural and reasonable," declared Civil War preacher Archibald Alexander, "for a dependent creature to apply to its Creator for what it needs, as for a child to solicit the aid of a parent who is believed to have the disposition and ability to bestow what it needs."

Although you can pray anytime and anywhere, it is helpful to have a daily discipline. Make an appointment with yourself to spend at least 5 minutes each day in prayer. I like to actually look over my calendar each week and schedule prayer times. I find it easier if I schedule it for the same time every day to keep in a routine. Take this appointment as seriously as you would any other appointment, and don't let interruptions keep you from this most important part of your day.

Prepare a prayer place for yourself. It could be a special chair, the corner of a sunroom, a window seat, or a spot in your bedroom. I keep a daily devotional book, journal, and pen together in a pretty wicker basket that I can carry to whichever room I am inspired to use for prayer. In the journal, I can record special prayer requests, answers to prayer, and the names of people I am praying for. Sometimes writing in my journal is a form of prayer in itself, helping to keep me focused.

When we were little, my sister and I knelt every night by our beds and recited the familiar child's prayer; "Now I lay me down to sleep. I pray the Lord my soul to keep. If I should die before I wake, I pray the Lord my soul to take." When my own children were of an age to start saying bedtime prayers, I hesitated to teach them that prayer. It sounded a bit morbid. Now I realize what a beautiful expression of faith it is to God. We can sleep in peace because He's the keeper of our souls—here on earth and when we die!

A simple formula for praying goes like this: Pray like it all depends on God; behave like it all depends on you. Most of all, pray believing. When you pray for rain, you'd better take your umbrella!

THE END OF
THE DAY

For the last time, good night!

think God gave us the gift of bedtime prayers with our children as a wonderful opportunity to make up for all the craziness that has gone on during the day. When we tuck our little ones into bed at night, say a prayer with them, and caress their tiny faces as they drift off into dreamland, we realize that it is worth all the effort, all the giving, all the tolerating, all the struggles, and all the sacrifices. With my own children, after they'd had their baths, had a bedtime snack and a story, said their prayers, and had good night hugs and kisses, I would often linger on the edge of their bed for a while, wondering if they would remember these precious times. Or, would they only remember the day their mother acted like a wild woman totally out of control because they had licked the icing from the freshly made carrot cake set aside for the makeup party that evening? Would they remember the Christmas I stayed up until 4 A.M. sewing red leather Barbie pants with legs that were narrower than a pencil and had to be turned inside out using a shish kabab skewer? Or the times I organized elaborate birthday parties with 20 or more of their school friends because nobody could be left out, and took the time to wrap nickels, dimes, and quarters in waxed paper and bake them right in their birthday cakes? Would they remember the times we jumped in piles of autumn leaves, or spent whole summer days at the wading pool while they hollered, "Mom, look at me!" the entire time? What about the winter picnics with bonfires, skating on the pond, trips to the library, a house full of their friends doing craft projects, and singing around the piano on Sunday afternoons? Would they cherish the memory of getting to stay up late on Saturday nights to play Snakes and Ladders, and laughing so hard at the dinner table one night that a mouthful of somebody's hot dog went airborne across the kitchen (we never did know whose it was) and we all fell backward off our chairs? Would they remember the time they were brokenhearted because their tiny kitten fell out of a tree and broke her leg, so Mommy prayed for her until she got better? Or would they remember a strict, stern mother who always flew off the handle over dirty clothes on the floor, capless shampoo bottles left to dribble down the side of the tub, curling irons left plugged in, and music so loud it set your teeth on edge? Would their memories be of a woman who dedicated her life to washing kitchen floors, vacuuming carpets, cleaning fingerprints from the refrigerator, urging them to stop talking with food in their mouths, and nagging them about keeping their rooms clean before the Salvation Army was called in to haul the junk away? Oh, how I hope they remember a mom who spent her mornings on her knees talking to God and her nights praying over them while they slept.

Tonight, as you tuck in your precious children, ask yourself about some of the memories you are making together. From this day forward, you can choose to build memories of warmth and happiness, innocent pleasures and simple delights, simplicity and serenity, laughter and love.

Last Christmas, I wrapped big, empty boxes in red and green foil gift wrap, added pretty ribbon and coordinating bows, and piled them on a bench to decorate our front porch. When our grandchildren saw them, their eyes were wide with delight and anticipation of what must be inside presents that size. Although we explained that the boxes were empty, the children clamored to unwrap them. When they were finally allowed to open them, how disappointed they were to see there was nothing inside. Sometimes our homes can be like those boxes—pretty to look at but lacking true substance inside. Your family is wanting to experience the real thing, only to find that you are too worn out, weary, and exhausted. Choose from this day on to nurture yourself. It is never too late to make midcourse corrections. Look after yourself and everything else will fall into place. I appreciate the words of Martin Luther King when he said, "My obligation is to do the right thing; the rest is in God's hands."

CONCLUSION

There's a Jewish proverb that says, "God could not be everywhere, therefore he created mothers." And ever since, mothers have been trying to be everywhere! When moms stop running on automatic pilot, when we step away from our harried schedules and packed calendars, we can begin to see that there is a world of wonder right at our fingertips. We begin to discover childlike contentment in the simple things. We become aware of our innermost longings—to experience simplicity and balance in our families, homes, and personal lives.

Nurturing yourself with 5-minute retreats is a way to infuse your life with joy so you go back to being a mom with a full heart rather than an empty one. When our children see us sacrificing for them at the expense of our own health and well-being, they are being taught that moms really don't have value. If they see us working hard to attain some of the material things in this world, they wonder if they have value. My friend Barry Spilchuk summed it all up when he wrote:

> The country clubs, the cars, the boats,
> Your assets may be ample.
> But the best inheritance you can leave your kids
> Is to be a good example.

239

My prayer for you is this:

Peace be both to thee, and peace be to thine house,
and peace be unto all that thou hast.

1 SAMUEL 25:6 KJV

Just one more word—please steal time every day, if you cannot find it any other way, to lie on the grass, or in a hammock under a huge tree...and relax. What a tonic this is for the soul! What a rest for weary nerves! Our husbands, children, friends—yes, and the nation—will profit by our relaxation. The greatest need today is for calmer homes, and no fireside can be calm unless its guardian is at peace with the world.

NELL B. NICHOLS, 1924